Making a Comprehensive Work

THE ROAD FROM BOMB ALLEY

Peter Dawson

Basil Blackwell · Oxford

First published in 1981 by
Basil Blackwell Publisher
108 Cowley Road
Oxford OX4 1JF
England

British Library Cataloguing in Publication Data

Dawson, Peter
    Making a Comprehensive Work.
    1. Eltham Green School
    I. Title.
    373.421'61

ISBN 0-631-12534-5
ISBN 0-631-12619-8 Pbk

Filmset by Getset (Bowden Typesetting Services) Ltd, Eynsham, Oxford.

Printed in Great Britain by Billing and Sons Ltd.
London, Guildford, Oxford and Worcester.

CONTENTS

Men are not made for safe havens

Aeschylus 500 BC

Preface

The greater part of this book was written in the autumn of 1979 during a sabbatical term at Corpus Christi College, Cambridge. It was completed in the spring of 1980 on the tenth anniversary of my arrival as Headmaster of Eltham Green School.

The chapters which follow are a review of the years 1970-80 and a description of the school's situation at the time of writing. The names of participants in this story have, of course, been changed wherever this was felt necessary. Doubtless some of the organizational features will have altered by the time these words are published, since the school will by then have passed into other hands following my departure to become General Secretary of the Professional Association of Teachers.

A change of leadership provides a stimulus in the life of any sizeable institution, and it is in my view desirable for the headship of a large comprehensive school to run for no more than a decade. There will be those who question that, together with many of the other claims and assertions contained between the covers of this book.

Said one young member of the Eltham Green staff to another, observing the Headmaster in company with his wife: 'Fancy having to *live* with him.' For my wife's support and forbearance during the events described in this book, and for her tireless enthusiasm in typing the manuscript, my warmest thanks.

Peter Dawson
April 1980

One

Initiation

'That', said the formidable lady teacher of catering, 'is your initiation.' From the window of my study, a set of exercise books could be seen descending from the fifth floor of the science block. Memory plays strange tricks, and it is unlikely they made their way downwards in slow motion, but that is how recollection tells the story.

The schoolkeeper had not cleared the terrace below the main teaching block during the holidays. He wanted the new headmaster to know how things really were. Broken desks and chairs, dispatched from the windows rising five storeys above, littered the paving stones. He explained: 'My men never come out here when the school's in session. Someone could get his skull smashed in.' This was Bomb Alley. No one – staff, pupils or cleaners – ever referred to the area by any other name.

A few weeks after my appointment, the Inner London Education Authority made clear their intention of reducing the size of the school. Plans had apparently been formulated for some time; it was no more than a recognition of the existing situation. Although the school had been designed to recruit thirteen forms of thirty pupils each autumn, giving an annual intake of 390 children from local primaries, there was immense difficulty in persuading parents to make the appropriate choice. Figures for the spring of 1970 showed a shortfall of four forms in first-choice applications for the coming autumn. It had been like that for years; the school had never received anything approaching a full complement except by filling up with boys and girls rejected from elsewhere. This had been especially true as far as those of high ability were concerned. After a government inspection of

1

the school in 1963, Her Majesty's Inspectors had noted in their report that the school had consistently received less than its anticipated quota of able pupils.

An assistant education officer sent down from County Hall to justify the impending decision was not well received by the school governors. They felt that cutting the school down to its recruitment size would be a further blow to its reputation. 'We assume,' said the chairman to me, 'that you are with us in fighting this.' But I was not. One of the school's principal problems arose from pressure on accommodation and, even more important, congestion in corridors, entrances and playgrounds. Anyone who denies that the large school generates problems of its own by its very size is blind to the obvious. This is especially true when the monster is out of control.

Looking back in the spring of 1979 and talking about how things had once been, a senior member of staff had this to say on *The London Programme* when London Weekend Television brought their cameras into the school: 'Life was very difficult . . . we had to try and control a class to silence them before we started teaching . . . the general discipline in the corridors was far worse than I've ever seen in any school at all. The children ran along, they pushed the staff aside, slammed doors in their faces . . . they used to zoom up and down five floors in the lifts and one couldn't do a thing about it.'

The notion that nothing could be done about it was, of course, false. But the attitude of mind leading to that conclusion infected the staff like a virus. It was exemplified by a disagreement that led to the departure of one of the most experienced members of the pastoral staff, whose reluctance to take a hard line with troublemakers appalled me. He was a man with limitless compassion for children with behaviour problems. Sadly this led him to pay less than adequate attention to the effect of the disruptive individual on ordinary children who simply wished to live in peace.

In his book *Robert Kennedy and his Times*, Arthur Schlesinger says of that extraordinary man: 'What he had in the way of weakness was an essential part of his strength.' The converse was also true, and this is a profound truth that applies to all of us. The seeds of our weaknesses lie in our strengths, and the basis of whatever is our main strength can be discerned in actions that show weakness. So determination becomes blind intransigence; imperturbability, fatal inaction. Especially, sympathy for the disadvantaged can become vulnerability to the opportunist.

It is a characteristic of some of those who work on the pastoral side in large schools that they allow concern for the miscreant to overrule all other considerations. It is an attitude also found among those who work in what are known as the supportive services. The destroyers they care so much about are given a degree of consideration that works to the disadvantage of the rest of the community. Never has so much been done for so few at the expense of so many. There is a sense in which the well-behaved boys and girls have become the disadvantaged children in our society.

At the school where my initiation into headship took place ten years ago, those children with an inclination to behave themselves needed some strength of character to hold fast to their intentions. In a classroom where disorder abounds, a perfectly normal boy with good manners will become rude and disruptive. In a playground where threats and taunts are the order of the day, those with no inclination to threaten or taunt will soon pick up the habit. Children seem to me much the same from generation to generation. They are exciting, infuriating, idle, tireless, open, scheming creatures – much like the adults whose passions create them. What they become depends on what we expect of them.

This may seem a truism, but it is nevertheless one that needs restating. If there is one generalization that can be accurately applied to education in England today, it is that we do not *expect* enough. Neither parents nor teachers have sufficient ambition for the young people in their care, either in regard to their academic achievements or their standards of behaviour.

Mrs Blake understood the purpose of schooling, even though one of the several sons she sent us was a real problem. 'I want you,' she declared, 'to learn 'em to read proper, write proper, add up proper and behave theirselves.' That unsophisticated analysis of what education should be about puts the truth in a nutshell. If every child were stretched to the limit in terms of literacy, numeracy and good behaviour, we would have something to be proud of in our education system.

This book is not history, nor is it educational philosophy, since I am competent to write neither. Perhaps it is a book about school management, although that too may seem presumptuous. It would be best to think of it simply as an account of a journey; a sort of pilgrimage during which one of London's largest and most splendidly built comprehensive schools emerged from a period of great difficulty, to earn from the local Member of Parliament an accolade in the House of Commons: 'It is worth reminding the House that in my constituency there is a comprehensive school which is oversubscribed in all ranges of ability.' If the story behind that is worth telling, this book is worth reading.

The questions it raises have to do with a wide range of educational issues, none of them more important than the changing position of the head teacher within our education system. In the middle of the seventies, the following appeared in *The Sunday Times* under the heading 'Headmasters Rule': 'The new corporation Headmaster can earn more than a junior Minister. In a large comprehensive he controls thousands of adolescents, hundreds of staff. He is a manager, educator, technocrat and politician.'

Many of those in charge of large schools would feel somewhat flattered by that. Christopher Chataway's account of the life of a Cabinet Minister, might seem more relevant:

> The two hallmarks of British Government over the last fifteen years have been its steadily increasing responsibility and its steadily diminishing power. A Minister today can much less often feel like the helmsman, with a vessel responding to his touch. The closer analogy all too often is surf-riding: a test of skill that is fascinating and all-absorbing but certain ultimately to be brought to an ignominious end by a wave that is too large.

> (*The Sunday Times*, 21 April 1974)

The notion that the headmaster of today in a very large school is some sort of educational mastermind, combining a rare blend of management skills with subtle political acumen, is altogether too grandiose – although pleasant to contemplate from the comfort and relative safety of a well-appointed study with an engaged sign showing at the door. Nearer to reality is an analysis that recognizes that we are only just beginning to understand how to organize and run such schools so that the processes of teaching and learning take precedence over the matter of survival. The financial investment which has been made in very large comprehensives, and the political commitment involved, together make it unthinkable that they should be dismantled. They are a permanent feature of education today and we have to come to terms with them.

There are, of course, those who believe that the monster comprehensive cannot work; that no man can lift its huge bulk above the level of the lowest standards of achievement and behaviour. It has been similarly alleged that, according to the theory of aerodynamics, the bumble bee cannot fly. The size, weight and shape of its body in relation to its wing span make flight impossible. But the bumble bee, being ignorant of these scientific facts, and possessing considerable determination, not only flies but makes honey too.

It will take another fifty years at least for the large comprehensive school to become a properly established and fully accepted element in our education system. We sometimes overlook the fact that it has taken centuries for our most famous schools to reach their present eminence. We expect too much if we believe an effective comprehensive system can be established in no more than a few decades.

I entered the teaching profession in the autumn of 1957, taking an appointment at a fine old grammar school which had its origin three centuries before, when the Stuarts ruled and misruled England. When I arrived at the school, there were four teachers on the staff who were able to claim between them two hundred years of acquaintance with the place as men and boys. It was, one might add, a somewhat conservative institution. Little did those four men, or indeed any of us, realize the destiny that lay in wait twenty years on. And when will that school be ready to be judged in its new comprehensive role? Given the same amount of time to mature as before, the answer is about the middle of the twenty-third century.

On 4 October in that autumn of 1957 when I began teaching, a new sound came across the airwaves: the bleep-bleep-bleep of the first Sputnik launched by the Russians. 'It seemed,' wrote Emmett John Hughes some time afterwards in *The Ordeal of Power* 'too quiet and well-modulated a voice for the Soviet Union to use to inform the world that the frontier of the space age had been crossed.'

But voices in the field of education were less muted. This was the time when most of London's large comprehensives were being built and opened. Kidbrooke had led the way in 1954, and others quickly followed. In the autumn of 1959, the London inspectorate carried out a survey of sixteen of its comprehensive schools, no fewer than six of which had opened in new buildings in the years 1955-57. The impetus towards the creation of a new system of education in the capital was at its height. There was no doubt in the minds of the political leadership that a new frontier was being crossed, and it was proclaimed with confidence.

While taking great pains to disclaim any premature judgements, the report by the inspectors carried a number of conclusions. Looking back from today's vantage point, three seem to be of special significance.

Firstly, the schools revealed – 'some clearly and others with less certainty' – that the new kind of secondary unit could not and should not be regarded as the old writ large. Some recognized the need for a new approach better than others. 'The message is clearest,' it was reported, 'in those schools which have entered with confidence into a new way of life.'

Secondly, the head teacher had a changed role in the new organization. His functions had, on the one hand, to do with policy and planning and, on the other, with internal and external relations. He was seen as a management figure first and an educator after that. Consultation and delegation were the key words.

Thirdly, the investigators had something to say about a subject that moved into the centre of the education debate in the seventies and threatens to dominate it in the eighties: 'There is a widespread awareness of the need for careful and even (*sic*) refined assessments of each pupil's potential.' The question of assessment is going to receive close attention from those who make educational policy for some time to come; but the London survey of 1959 did not have in mind what is being talked about today. The quantification of potential is now seen as far less critical than the need to monitor achievement. The story of why and how that has happened tells us a good deal about the outcome of the new secondary system. We are now quite good at establishing a pupil's potential. What we have not yet discovered is how to bring it to fruition. At the present time, this is particularly true of the average child. In his autobiography, *Diary of a Maverick*, Maurice Wiggin describes his own experience as a child at a small country school. In winter, the clever children were alright because they were allowed to sit at the back by the hot water pipes. The backward youngsters were also taken care of, because they had to sit at the front and the boiler was situated there. The ones who suffered were the poor little perishers in the middle. It is thus in the large comprehensive at the beginning of the eighties. In the last decade great care and considerable resources were devoted to meeting the needs of the children at the extremes of ability. If they are neglected, the consequences are quickly obvious. But there are thousands of young people of middle ability who get away with seven out of ten but are capable of eight if only they were taught better, pressed harder, given more attention. Not that they will thank me for saying so. No one is bothering them and they are not bothering anyone else. They do not wish their teachers to take too much interest in how much reading they are doing, how long they are spending on homework and that sort of thing. Perhaps the eighties will be the decade in which our education system begins to devote a proper share of its attention to the needs of the ordinary, average child. If so, it will take a major step forward in tapping the nation's greatest resource.

The three conclusions drawn in 1959 had a precise relevance to the condition of Eltham Green School at the time of my arrival in April 1970. Its academic organization was derived from the grammar school, as was its examination entry policy. The functions of the headmaster had the same basis and took little account of management techniques, most notably in the important area of external relations. There was no significant provision for those children of least potential. These three fatal flaws detracted from the school's achievements. Its reputation in the community was appalling.

Three specific areas of activity summed up the situation and revealed the heart of the school's problems.

The academic structure combined broad banding across three levels of ability with streaming within each band. This produced a category of child spoken of dismissively as a C4. A third-year boy was sent out of a lesson for misbehaviour. Staffroom comment: 'He's a C.' End of discussion. To earn such a title was to be regarded by many as unteachable. Precisely the same attitude prevailed in the traditional grammar school towards children in the bottom stream, regardless of the fact that they were of very high potential; and it continues to prevail where such schools still exist. An analysis of the examination results of the bottom streams in the country's grammar schools over the last twenty-five years would reveal a disaster area that has been carefully and deliberately hidden from view.

The policy for examination entries was similarly based on grammar school tradition, the GCE being regarded as the only worthwhile examination to take. The statistics for just one year told the story: 849 entries for O level produced only 367 passes in 1970. Of the 482 failures, thirty per cent were at the lowest grade, indicating that the candidates' answers were abysmal.

Without doubt the school's poor reputation derived in part from the lack of any systematic attempt at an external relations policy. There was, indeed, considerable suspicion of any outside interest in the school. It was perhaps a pity that the 1959 report did not spell out more clearly its conclusions on this subject. It has taken schools too long to realize that, given the development of public and political interest in education, they are — to use a fashionable phrase — a legitimate source of investigation. We have to come to terms with this, like it or not.

Fortuitously, the centenary of the Forster Education Act and the establishment of the London School Board coincided with my appointment. This encouraged me to hold an open day and to invite not only parents but a wide range of community interests to come and see what really went on inside our doors. If people's worst suspicions were confirmed, little had been lost. On the other hand, the truth might prove our friend, which is how it turned out. From that time onwards, we have always had fair treatment from the media and other interests. Not that the apprehensions of those connected with the school were quickly dispelled. When a local newspaper wrote an article some time later on our out-of-school activities, it was headlined: 'The Things they do at Eltham Green'. This brought an immediate telephone call from one of the governors who wanted to know what on earth those newspaper people had got hold of now. It turned out he had not actually read the article but only the headline.

The changes that overtook Eltham Green School in the seventies had at their heart something of a paradox. The thirty or so members of staff who resigned at the end of my first term were in the main of progressive disposition. A significant figure among them was an English specialist who subsequently published a novel about life in a large comprehensive school in which, at the outset, the headmaster dropped dead in his private toilet. The paradox attending the apparent conflict between myself and the progressives lay in the fact that my philosophy was regarded by many observers as forward-looking and liberal. The exception was my view of discipline — a subject so emotive as to dominate all other considerations and overthrow rational judgement.

One of the greatest problems facing the head teacher of any large school is that of being categorized in general terms on the basis of chosen policy on a particular issue. For example, it was once suggested in my hearing that schools that do not have a uniform are not much concerned about academic standards. It is fatally easy to feel bound to conform to the category in which one is placed. Having been described by Bruce Kemble of the *Daily Express* as the toughest headmaster in Britain, there was a temptation to try and live up to the title. The threat this presented to dispassionate judgement is hard to exaggerate. There are many schools that would break out of the mould in which they have been cast by parents, politicians and the media, given half the chance.

But these considerations were far from my mind when, with a sense of apprehension not diminished by those exercise books floating down from the fifth floor of the science block, I assumed responsibility for Eltham Green School.

There was a long road ahead, but no doubt in my mind that what mattered most on setting out was that there should be confidence in the leadership, and that the leadership should appear confident. Theodore White, the American political journalist, has made an analysis of government which is relevant to the business of running a large school. It is as if a great company of people have embarked upon an immense journey:

> The country ahead is full of unknown dangers and fresh promise . . . In the procession there are those who trudge on foot, those who ride in the wagons, those who go by horse. On and on they go . . . some infuriated by the slowness of the pace, and others who insist the journey pause because the pace is too fast . . . Up there at the head of the advance column, the leaders quarrel bitterly among themselves . . . They disagree as to what course to take, at what pace, at what cost. They know that much later they will be judged by some archaeologist's description of their route, of their perception, their decision. But they know that now, right now, they can hold on to their leadership not by largeness of vision or logic of plan but only by the judgement and approval of those who follow . . . (*The Making of the President. 1964*).

The approval of those who follow, or at least their acquiescence, is essential to the success of the educational exercise we call running a school. Staff, pupils and parents must believe in what is happening and feel themselves to be part of it. In practical terms, this means first and foremost believing in the leadership. If such belief exists, all will move as one.

Professor Michael Rutter's research into the workings of secondary schools gets to the heart of the matter. He shows that what makes for success is not that a school should have a particular form of organization but that it should possess a clearly defined ethos as a social institution.

The same idea was expressed in the mid-seventies by Trevor Jaggar, at that time Inspector for Secondary Education with the Inner London Education Authority and now its Chief Inspector (Schools). Speaking on the subject 'What are the Characteristics of a Good School?', he claimed that successful schools were those with what he called coherent and manifest styles, where the purposes of the institution – and the intended means of achieving them – were clear to staff, children and parents. In the pages which follow, I hope the particular style that emerged at Eltham Green School between 1970 and 1980 will become clear, each chapter telling one aspect of the story.

The terrace below the main teaching block has been free of smashed furniture and similar missiles for some years now. That particular problem was not difficult to resolve. Staff, parents and pupils would now regard it as unthinkable for behaviour leading to that sort of thing to be tolerated. But other changes of attitude have taken longer; it has not been a swift or easy road from Bomb Alley.

Two

Discipline

Speaking at a conference of head teachers in the summer of 1977, Sheila Browne, Senior Chief Inspector of Schools at the Department of Education and Science, said that what dictates action in a school is not so much what is actually going on but what people think is going on, the impression of how things are. Significantly, the gathering at which she made this remark was concerned among other things with control in schools. Her own particular contribution was entitled 'Raising Educational Standards'.

The speaker had no particular knowledge of the Eltham Green situation as it had been at the beginning of the seventies, but her observation fitted it like a glove. It was the opinion of a significant number of senior staff, and of a great many people in the Eltham community, that the school was out of control. That view was shared at official level and had helped to determine my appointment. This impression of how things were overrode all other considerations and dominated people's thinking. One could, of course, have adopted the attitude of the Irish rugby coach Syd Millar. In 1975, faced with the prospect of defeat against England, he observed that his situation was desperate but not serious. There were some people connected with the school who seemed inclined to take a similar view. My own inclinations were less sanguine.

The principal need was to bring to an end the rule of the ruffian. The other changes that were called for, and that have been referred to in the previous chapter, would be ineffective until the school was made safe for teachers and taught. When this had been achieved, a girl said to me in my study, 'I'd like to come here. I think I will be safe.' She was not a frightened eleven-year-old brought by her parents from a local primary school. She was a young woman applying for a teaching post, and it is a sad comment on our education system that there are new young teachers searching for schools where they will not be abused and threatened.

'The art of leadership,' said President Harry S. Truman, 'is persuading people to do what they should have done in the first place.' The trouble is, if people fail to do in the first place what needs doing, sterner measures are required later. There was a dramatic escalation in the use of corporal punishment on my arrival at Eltham Green, made necessary by the condition of the school. It was as objectionable to me as to everyone else, although that was something that it would have been quite unthinkable to make known. It made for an unpleasant start, and necessarily brought me into conflict with teachers (some had no problems in the classroom and could not see why others had), parents (usually the ones who wanted that bully over there thrashed but never their own child), and politicians. The inspectorate, as was and is their custom, simply observed the situation.

The extent of what happened was measurable, and the statistics for the period 1970-71 were in due course placed beside those of earlier years for the benefit of the school governors. They showed that the cane had been used on average 28 times a term during the three years immediately prior to my appointment, while it was used 169 times in my first term and 145 times in my second term. The report that went along with these figures contained the following observations:

On their own, statistics of corporal punishment mean very little. They need to be related to other factors, in particular the state of discipline within a school. There has been a massive decline in the rate of damage within the building, a more orderly atmosphere for teachers to operate in and some progress in the matter of the school's reputation among people who live nearby. These developments have made worthwhile the time and energy which has been devoted to catching and punishing those who would wreck the school and its name.

There were those on the staff who seemed to think the advent of a new régime had actually given rise to the introduction of corporal punishment, but that was certainly not the case. Its more extensive use simply reflected a much higher rate of catching miscreants. Escalation therefore brought with it a greater degree of justice.

If corporal punishment is to be retained in English schools, head teachers must be free to use it as extensively as the occasion demands without having to worry about the score. Failing that, injustice is inevitable. The notion that caning is defensible provided it is used only a little has no basis in logic or morality. The abolitionists have by far the better of the argument when it is carried on at that level.

There is a perfectly good case to be made for the use of the cane, but is has nothing to do with *how much* it is used. It is a sanction which some have found quick, effective and morally inoffensive. That is a matter of fact, however much some would argue *they* do not find it either of the last two things. Furthermore, regard should be given to the views of parents who want corporal punishment to be available in the schools to which the state compels them to send their children.

But abolition does not matter nearly as much as some imagine. It is not important which rewards and punishments are available, but how they are used. If that were not the case, how is it that schools taking very similar children and using much the same behavioural controls so frequently show different results? The answer is in the leadership and quality of teachers. Schools that are determined to have good behaviour will get it somehow, no matter what sanctions are available or forbidden.

One of the difficulties in the whole area of punishments is that there are objections to so many of them. Suspension is under attack because it puts troublemakers on the streets where they break the law. Detention is frowned upon, especially when it means children making their way home alone on dark winter evenings. There are more complaints from parents about that than there have ever been about corporal punishment. Written impositions are dying out since it has at last occurred to the teaching profession that it is self-defeating to encourage children to write and then use writing as a punishment. Not letting those who wreck the dining hall have any dinner is, according to the Child Poverty Action Group, going too far. Making girls scrub the school steps has been described to me as evidence of sadistic tendencies. One is left looking forward with interest to the day when the growing army of inspectors and advisers addresses itself to this question and makes some practical suggestions.

Many of the alternatives to swift and straightforward retribution call upon teachers to give more of their time to the disruptive element and less to the ordinary child. Counselling children, keeping them in, making them carry out tasks about the school, setting them extra work, calling in their parents – these and many more ways of bringing children into line require the teacher to remove his attention from the well-behaved child and devote it to the miscreant, sometimes at very great length. The declared policy of the Society of Teachers Opposed to Physical Punishment is to encourage 'counselling, withdrawal and referral' of disruptive pupils. The demands these alternatives make upon the financial and staffing resources of the nation are massive. In 1978, Inner London announced proposals to spend one and a half million pounds on measures to deal with disruptive pupils. In November 1979, the Director of Education (Schools) informed a conference of teachers gathered to discuss truancy and disruption that spending on a variety of solutions had reached two and a half millions per annum.

A great deal of the money was devoted to the creation of off-site support centres, which have become the new growth area in education. The centres have teacher-pupil ratios well below one teacher to ten children and make nonsense of all those arguments about GCE A level groups being too small. Unless, that is, you think the needs of the wrecker are greater than those of the university entrant. There is some evidence that the debate is drifting in precisely that direction. Our education system is removing itelf further and further from the needs of the ordinary child who wants to work hard and pass examinations. When is there to be an extra injection of resources for the boys and girls who actually *like* school and who do not practise abuse on their teachers?

The extent of teacher abuse and violence at Eltham Green School at the end of the sixties was frightening. Entries in the punishment book were frank and specific, although they only showed the tip of the iceberg. One boy had called his mathematics teacher 'a fucking little cunt'. Another had told his metalwork master he was a bastard. A female teacher had been hit by a boy 'in a struggle for an elastic band'. One boy was punished for 'launching himself' at a teacher, another for 'putting in the boot'.

The schoolkeeper insisted on having the toilets redecorated before taking me round them. Some were still barely usable. Damage to fittings was widespread, and it took over a year to put most things right. It is an area in which there will always be problems, and it would be dishonest to pretend they were eliminated. But there *is* a way of maintaining reasonable standards. The key is vigilance. It is the responsibility of *all* the teachers in a school to contribute to this.

Many contributed by assuming what were called Posts of Very Special Responsibility. A team of teachers was made responsible for each of the toilets in the school. Each had to be thoroughly inspected at least once in the morning and once in the afternoon. This meant going right in and having a proper look round, not just a quick glance through the outside door. Two principal things had to be looked out for: scribbling on walls and damage to bolts and catches on cubicles. It was made clear how to get graffiti removed and damage repaired. I drew up the duty schedule personally and kept a very close eye on its implementation. Toilet training became a key area in the school curriculum. The state of the lavatories in a school correlates closely with examination results.

Critics may say that a headmaster should not have to spend his time on the guardianship of the ablutions, that he should not make himself keeper of the water closets. But sometimes he has to, because his chief function is to create conditions in which the teaching process may prosper. It most certainly cannot if the corridors are being flooded because of vandalized plumbing. 'I did not,' said one teacher, 'come into teaching to be inspecting toilets all the time.' That was someone who had not been trained properly; someone who did not know what professionalism is all about. There is *nothing* that goes on inside a school that is not the professional responsibility of the teaching team working in it. Everything that happens is of a piece.

Ordinary people understand these simple things. A couple of years ago, when we had an open day in connection with eleven-plus transfers, I came across a man examining the doors. Not wanting to discourage his interest in the school fabric, I nevertheless asked if he would like a sixth-former to take him round to see some lessons in progress. No, he did not need that. He could find out what he needed to know from the state of the doors. He was the carpenter at a local comprehensive and could tell a good school by the way it was looked after.

Windows were the biggest problem. They were being smashed at the rate of seventeen a month. At a minimum of £20 each, that came to £4000 a year, which was a great deal of money in 1970. In fact, anything above the first floor required the scaffolder as well as the glazier and could cost £50 or more. It was an architectural feature that no window could be replaced by working from inside. Most vulnerable were the glass doors at the entrances. A quick thrust with a boot was a recognized way of expressing dissatisfaction with the education system in general and being told off last lesson in particular. Again, vigilance – together with dreadful retribution – provided the answer. Catch one villain and deal with him firmly, and you will discourage ten others. It became quickly established that a good hiding and paying up were the inevitable consequences of breaking a window. Leaving room for accidents, the first part of the retribution did not apply if you owned up and thereby saved the headmaster the trouble of doing his own detective work. Of course, the demand for payment could not be supported in law.

But parents accepted it as natural justice. On only one occasion did a parent refuse to cooperate, and he was a police officer who knew his rights and insisted on them. We simply withdrew his son from lessons and made him clean windows until he had earned the cost of the one he smashed.

Boots were banned on the grounds that some kinds were little short of offensive weapons. This led to some amusing situations. A fourth-year boy who insisted on wearing his steel-capped 'cherries' was confronted in the corridor and made to remove them. Walking round in stockinged feet all day, he attracted the attention of his mates who insisted on stamping on his toes at every opportunity. After limping home that night in his socks, he wore shoes. His boots remained in my cupboard and were never claimed.

Two features of the building required attention in the interests of good discipline. Four ornamental ponds situated in front of the main doors provided a temptation some children simply could not resist. Those about to leave school were pushed in as a sort of valedictory gesture by their friends. The ponds were filled in and that was the end of the problem. The builders also gave me a window in my study looking out towards the main gate. The lack of one was an open invitation to intruders.

These two matters serve to underline a general feature of the architecture of many large and expensively-built schools. Those who design them seem to have little or no idea of the practicalities of day-to-day life in such institutions. It was the constant complaint of E. G. Hughes, the first headmaster of Liverpool's pioneer comprehensive at Gateacre, that no one ever came back after the building was opened to see if it worked. If a little more attention were given to school design, a great many disciplinary problems could be eliminated. The sort of building in which a child has to live his school life can and does have a powerful effect on his behaviour.

Along with the window I had installed went a pair of high-powered binoculars. These enabled me to identify the local villains hanging about the gate. Knowing who is about to invade you is a fairly sure way of knowing what sort of trouble to expect. The binoculars were also useful for determining which of our boys were going into the neighbouring girls' school by climbing the fence in the park on the other side of the road. One boy was nonplussed when he was sent for at afternoon registration and confronted with my knowing about his misbehaviour. 'Do you know how I found you out?' I asked. He thought perhaps I had been hiding up a tree, or spying from the park keeper's hut. When I showed him my binoculars and explained that I had been watching him from the school roof, he was clearly impressed. He felt it necessary to warn everyone of the situation without delay, which served my purpose very well. The binoculars are not used very much these days, but from time to time I wander round the grounds in the lunch hour with them in my hand.

Probably the most important weapon introduced into the disciplinary armoury was the red card system. This was simply an extension of the traditional lesson report system used in most schools, whereby children who misbehave have to carry round with them a sheet of paper on which each teacher throughout the day provides a comment. Being on report is not liked, but some systems are more effective than others. The weakness of many is that the miscreant knows what his teachers have written before the senior member of staff who placed him on report. Furthermore, some apprehensive probationers are more inclined to write a good report if Big Terry is standing over them flexing his muscles and glowering with hatred, than if they are able to submit something confidential. Mean Mandy can be an even more frightening proposition. The ability of a sullen fourteen-year-old girl to intimidate a young teacher, especially one of her own sex, leaves the boys way behind.

The red card which was introduced is similar in size and appearance to that used by football referees. The miscreant has to present it to his teacher at the beginning of each lesson and retrieve it at the end. Staff carry special report pads for use when a red card is shown. When a pupil hands over his red card at the end of the day or first thing next morning to whoever issued it, there is a set of confidential reports waiting. This is the moment when he answers for his sins, including any he thought he had got away with.

Placing children on report is certainly not new, but the particular features of the report system introduced at Eltham Green in the seventies made it more effective than some used in other schools. There was a new refinement in 1980 when red badges were added. In certain circumstances, a pupil will be made to wear a badge to signify to the whole school that he is carrying a card. From time to time potential miscreants are reminded that both are the colour of blood.

The red card system received a good deal of national publicity, and there was criticism of spending on this rather than more important items. It is expensive, but its effectiveness makes our other investments worthwhile. There is no point in purchasing thirty textbooks for a class if the behaviour of one or two pupils threatens to bring the educational process to a halt. A classroom full of miscreants is very rare. When it does occur, it is a comment on the teacher or the academic organization of the school rather than on the children. Most trouble in lessons is caused by one or two disruptives. Identify and control them, and that carefully prepared lesson will work. Only then does the investment of time and resources in it prove worthwhile.

One boy's blood was actually spilled on the wall outside my study. He was a small West Indian with a mercurial temper. He gave us a lot of trouble but provided one excellent service. One day while stationed outside my study – where he spent most of his career with us – he happened to have a cut finger. It was not serious and he had not bothered to cover it, so a few drops of blood dripped on to the wall. At the end of the day, the cleaner was about to wash it off when I stopped her. It remained there for several weeks as a visual aid to miscreants. My deputies and I were able to offer clear evidence of just how far we were prepared to go. It became widely known throughout the school and beyond that there was actually blood on the wall in the headmaster's corridor at Eltham Green.

As has always been the case, and will always remain so, the girls were more difficult to bring under control than the boys. A high proportion of female troublemakers have fathers who ally themselves with their daughters in the hope of establishing a good relationship with them. It is a way of buying goodwill that inevitably backfires in the long run. The disruptive teenage female is a shrewd and cunning creature with a profound contempt for anyone who is a soft touch. More than one gullible parent has been brought face to face with a new and unpleasant reality when shown what his daughter has written on the toilet wall.

The belief in a better future evokes the effort and determination to bring it about. In the early seventies, it was essential for the staff at Eltham Green to take an optimistic view of the possibility of putting a stop to the wreckers and destroyers. Catching the troublemakers, and making it known that they had been caught and dealt with, therefore became an important priority in my day-to-day timetable.

A police officer once made the simple but profound point to me that no one commits a crime except on the assumption he will not be caught. If criminals believed in the inevitability of detection, there would be little crime, regardless of the penalties.

Children who smash doors, write obscenities on walls, start fires under the school pavilion, threaten those smaller than themselves with knives – and we had all of this and more – do these things believing they will get away with them. Once they know they will be caught, they stop. It was for that reason I gave so much time to touring the premises during my first couple of years of headship, and to announcing in corridors, classrooms, assembly hall and staffroom, 'I may be a rotten headmaster, but I'm a good detective.' Everybody believed the first proposition; if they could be led to believe the second as well, we were on the way to salvation.

I came to be much attracted by the motto of RAF Bomber Command: 'Strike Hard, Strike Sure'. I would simply wish to add, 'Strike First'.

The need to be tough with offenders did not arise simply from conditions within the school. The sixties was a time when, in the matter of young people's behaviour, western society reaped what it had sown. The fruits of permissiveness could be seen in schools and universities – and on the streets – on both sides of the Atlantic.

After a year, the time came to review the disciplinary situation. To that end, a commission on discipline was set up with the following terms of reference:

> To consider the ILEA document *Discipline in Schools*; to comment both in general and in particular with regard to Eltham Green School; to report and make recommendations to the Headmaster.

The ILEA document referred to had appeared in the autumn of 1970. While acknowledging a growing concern about indiscipline in secondary schools, the chief purpose of this fourteen-page report was to underline the desirability of abolishing corporal punishment. Obsession with this meant that only one of the fifty-one paragraphs on rewards and punishments was devoted to alternative sanctions. In consequence, it had little practical help to offer teachers working in schools. There was one crumb to be found at the end: 'The decision as to the conduct of his school in relation to its internal organization and its disciplinary methods is that of the headmaster.' That crumb has since been removed.

The sixteen teachers who accepted invitations to serve on the commission were selected to represent all shades of opinion and a wide range of experience. They spent a year on their task, and at the end of that time the fourteen who still remained on the staff produced a sixty-three page report. Their deliberations had been based not only on a great number of meetings among themselves and with others, but also on a lengthy questionnaire to all staff, and visits to other schools to see what they were doing about discipline. There were six main recommendations:

1   The majority opinion is that corporal punishment, no matter how abhorrent to some, is a necessary means of dealing with certain types of misdemeanour and acts as an effective deterrent upon many boys.

2   Inexperienced teachers need much more help, guidance and support from their more senior and experienced colleagues in dealing with disciplinary matters.

3   The need to help pupils to be not only gainfully occupied but interested is an important factor in establishing good order and discipline. This has been achieved effectively at Eltham Green School by the establishment of the social education department which has obviated many of the previous disciplinary problems posed by the more difficult fourth-year pupils.

4   There must always be close liaison between school and parents on disciplinary matters.

5   Although many refuse to admit it, there are many special problems presented by immigrant children (these lessen with the succeeding generations). Many of these pupils tend to be more excitable and less willing to accept correction and reprimand. There is also the very real problem of language difficulties with some.

6   Any system of punishment must be offset by a corresponding system of rewards.

The third conclusion was a reference to the establishment of a new department in the school soon after my arrival, of which more later; the fifth proved the most contentious and led in due course to the establishment of a commission on immigrant children.

Public reaction to the report was predictable. Both *The Times* and *The Guardian* commended the school for undertaking the investigation; the *Evening News* asked children what they thought about it; the local press concentrated on the corporal punishment issue; STOPP attacked the device of setting up an *ad hoc* committee and described the tone of the report as immoderate. Doubtless the creation of the committee would have been seen as more enlightened had it come to different conclusions.

In the event, the two most important recommendations turned out to be numbers two and three, which had to do with advice and support for inexperienced teachers on the one hand

and the structure of academic provision on the other. In short, there was need for two things: better guidance for staff, and more appropriate courses for children. Better teaching and a better curriculum were the keys to a better future.

A good deal of progress had already been made in the field of discipline before the report was published. This was reflected in a variety of areas, not least in the growing popularity of the school: there were almost a hundred more applicants for places in 1972 than there had been in 1970. Our eventual destiny in this regard had its amusing side. Only after our official form-entry had been reduced from thirteen to eleven did we start to recruit enough children to fill thirteen forms. By 1974 Eltham Green was oversubscribed for the first time in its history.

A large comprehensive school which is in difficulties will only change direction if there is dramatic action. It is no good, for example, making announcements in assembly about people showing more respect for their teachers or behaving on the buses. One must go out and collar the culprits, for all to see. That way, and that way only, is the message communicated. Communication is always the biggest problem in a large comprehensive school. That is true at all levels of the organization, from knowing where Johnny Jenkins is at this moment to knowing what the headmaster's policy is on teaching high flyers. One of the marks of a school in serious trouble is that communication breaks down. People aren't sure what is happening; what is supposed to be going on; which things matter and which things do not. In that situation, the headmaster has to put on a performance big enough for all to see. It is not, of course, a natural way to behave. There are no two professions more closely allied than teaching and acting. Especially in the field of discipline – in determining how children shall behave – dramatic gestures are sometimes required. If there was nothing else, there was drama at Eltham Green during its metamorphosis.

Three

Timetable and Curriculum

The way teaching is organized is invariably reflected in the attitudes and behaviour patterns of those receiving it. The style and ethos of a school depend to a large extent on timetable structure, and on the numerous decisions and assumptions that contribute to it. A school's philosophy may be seen more clearly in the nature of its curriculum and the way it is applied than in its public pronouncements. The head teachers of large comprehensives are much given to bold claims about stretching the able child, supporting those with learning difficulties, offering a broad range of options, and so on. The passion with which we make our assertions may perhaps indicate a degree of inner doubt. However that may be, the truth will out. The way boys and girls regard the world of school in which they spend fifteen thousand hours of their lives; how they treat their teachers and their peers; how they dress and walk about and speak to one another – these things inevitably and inexorably deliver a verdict on what is taught and how it is taught in the classroom. Any attempt to divorce the way children behave from the teaching process is blindness and self-deception; and yet teachers do it all the time, saying things like, 'If only that class knew how to behave, I would be able to teach them something.' Marcel Proust was right: the facts of life do not penetrate to the sphere in which our beliefs are cherished. If ordinary children persistently misbehave in and out of class, we need to look at what we are offering them. Which is not to say it is all up to the classroom teacher. More important are those decisions about the nature of teaching groups that are made before anyone closes the door on himself and his thirty pupils and faces the challenge and opportunity of a lifetime. If some of the decisions were made with greater care, fewer young teachers would find the classroom a disaster area.

Of course, there are numerous other influences at work that occasionally override the impact of teaching arrangements. The situation at home may dominate a particular pupil's performance; a whole year group can be affected by what Harry the Boot says he is going to do to Big John behind the gym at morning break (or by what he claims he did to Sally Easy over in the field last night); in a large school, the paralytic effect of rumour on the education process is well known. But all these influences are departures from the norm. Generally speaking, what determines the day-to-day, week-by-week lifestyle adopted by the great body of ordinary boys and girls in a school is what they are offered in their lessons. It is for education in the classroom that they are by force of law brought together and they know it. They also know we have them under false pretences if our arrangements fail to meet their needs. Assuming that effective teachers are available, the quality of provision will be determined by timetable and curriculum.

In the spring of 1970, each year group in the lower school at Eltham Green was divided into thirteen registration groups based on a house system and fourteen teaching groups determined by ability. The arrangement of teaching groups combined banding and streaming. It cannot be exactly represented by the notation system recommended for use in London schools which is illustrated in Table 1. On entry, the 390 children in a year group were separated into three ability bands, each of which followed a somewhat different programme of subjects. There was then a further subdivision into streams (see Table 2).

Within each band, pupils were taught in their streams by some departments but setted out into subject ability groups by others. The whole thrust of the timetable structure was therefore in the direction of separating children one way or another in terms of academic potential, or lack of it. It was not, of course, possible to practise mixed ability teaching. This was particularly regretted by the English staff at that time, who committed to

Table 1: Displaying the Curriculum: A Common Notation for Secondary Schools

Streaming		Banding		Mixed Ability		Parallel Banding with Streaming		Parallel Banding with Mixed Ability	
1A	30	1A1	30	1R	28	1A1	30	1C	28
1B	30	1A2	30	1Q	29	1B1	30	1J	28
1C	30	1A3	30	1B	27	1C1	30	1M	28
1D	30	1A4	30	1T	28	1D1	30	1D	27
1E	30	1B1	30	1H	27	1E1	30	1F	28
1F	30	1B2	30	1L	29	1F1	23	1Y	28
1G	30	1B3	30	1N	28	1G1	22	1P	28
1H	30	1B4	30	1V	27	1A2	30	1S	28
1I	30	1B5	30	1S	27	1B2	30	1E	28
1J	25	1B6	30	1W	28	1C2	30	1L	28
1K	25	1C1	23	1A	29	1D2	30	1R	27
1L	24	1C2	23	1P	28	1E2	30	1F	28
1M	23	1C3	22	1N	27	1F2	23	1W	28
1N	23	1C4	22	1Y	28	1G2	22	1Q	28

—————— Separates streams or bands

.... Separates groups each of which have the same spectrum of ability

= = = = Separates two halves of a year population each half containing a full spectrum of ability

Derived from a publication of the same title by the Inner London Education Authority, 1979. Adjusted to represent a school intake of 390 pupils divided into fourteen teaching groups.

Table 2: Teaching Groups, Spring 1970

1A1	30	
1A2	30	
1A3	30	
1A4	30	
1A5	30	
1B1	30	
1B2	30	
1B3	30	
1B4	30	
1B5	30	
1C1	25	
1C2	25	
1C3	20	
1C4	20	

═══════ Separates bands

─────── Separates streams within bands

writing their view that the great mass of children from A3 to C2 were much the same. While in its way encouraging, this also served to confirm one's suspicion that the staff regarded some children – especially those in C3 and C4 – as being unlike the rest of the human race.

While some remedial provision was made for children carrying the C3 and C4 label, no one pretended it was adequate. 'What', asked the deputy head, 'are we going to do about the Cs?' The same question, uttered with genuine anxiety by many of the best teachers in the school, was raised over and over again. The very fact that some children were thought of as 'the Cs' was the beginning of a disaster story. But the real disasters did not come at the beginning. Only when the children concerned moved into the upper school and found themselves once again offered not bread but a stone, did they take the law into their own hands. Given a public examination curriculum in the bottom sets in every subject, plus some extra time in the workshops or cookery rooms – the former were known as 'the sheds' – they became what everyone already knew they were: layabouts and trouble-makers. Father Dolan, the prefect of studies in James Joyce's *Portrait of the Artist as a Young Man*, would have recognized them at once as belonging to what he called the lazy idle loafers. To repeat myself: the way teaching is organized is invariably reflected in the attitudes and behaviour patterns of those receiving it.

It would be well to pause at this point and identify a problem that is found in every school and that defies solution. If one is to provide for the different needs of pupils of varying abilities, they must be separated from one another for some of their classroom time. But once that is done, two difficulties arise. Firstly, those who are separated because they are slow at learning acquire a stigma, while those who are separated because they are faster than the rest think of themselves as a superior form of creation. Secondly, all the separation systems available have what might be called a propensity to petrify. Except in the very short run, children tend not to be moved from the groups in which they are first placed. The teaching profession long ago acquired mastery of the art of fulfilling its own prophecies about children. What we decide boys and girls are capable of will be what they show themselves capable of. Organizational factors also act to restrict flexibility. Once a school timetable has been launched, pupils can only be moved between teaching groups by exchange. Furthermore, those of one level of ability may be following a different curriculum from those of another so that, by the time the school year has run through one term, movement between the two becomes unthinkable.

There are those who see mixed ability teaching as the way out of the dilemma. In their book *Half Way There*, Mrs Caroline Wedgwood Benn and Professor Brian Simon prescribe the abolition of all forms of streaming and all practices involving segregation of pupils as a necessary condition for the establishment of a genuinely comprehensive system of education. But even if it were true that unstreamed classes would solve the problem, they call for a kind of teacher not yet readily available in the secondary sector. The skill required to teach a mathematical high-flyer in the same class as a pupil who finds basic numeracy beyond him is uncommon among those who enter the profession. The attempt to solve the segregation problem by recourse to mixed ability teaching has driven some good teachers out of the classroom. The current shortage of linguists is in part the result of the rejection by many schools of streaming and setting. Teachers of foreign languages are inclined to be highly specialized. They are frequently so dedicated to their subject that they only want to work with children who show some definite signs of linguistic ability. When required to teach a foreign language to eleven-year-olds with reading ages of five or six, they lose heart. This is accelerated if they are expected to handle such children at the same time and in the same classes as youngsters who are capable of learning fast and are eager to press on. The present serious shortage of modern linguists in our schools arises naturally from the spread of the comprehensive system and mixed ability teaching.

Three of the arguments commonly advanced in favour of unstreamed classes deserve attention. Firstly, they are seen as a means of engineering a high level of social integration. Secondly, they allegedly overcome the damage to staff relationships caused by streaming. Thirdly, they reduce discipline problems.

It is questionable whether or not mixed ability classes have any effect on children's attitudes to one another. My own experience of working in an entirely unstreamed comprehensive in Liverpool convinced me that it was as easy for the least able child to be denigrated in that situation as in any other. Conversely, there are schools that segregate children for teaching purposes where relationships are of the highest order. But even if this were not so, any professional educator must question the validity of using a particular style of teaching as a means of reorganizing the social structure. Our first priority should be to ensure that children learn as much as possible while they undergo compulsory schooling, and we should be looking for the best way of bringing that about. Which is not to say that relationships do not matter and social integration is merely a fashionable notion to be shelved like many others. Go into the classroom of a really good teacher and his work will be reflected not only in what the children know but in the way they feel about and act towards one another. This is not achieved by insisting on particular teaching methods but by raising the standard of entry to the profession. If we want children to have a balanced view of the world, we need to look at the people we put in front of them.

In some schools it used to be a common practice for the most senior members of staff to teach the top groups in a streamed or setted situation while the young probationers cut their teeth – or learnt the art of survival – on the common herd. That was my own experience as a young grammar school teacher. The assumption was that one could do less harm to the no-hopers who were hardly worth bothering about than to the academic cream on whose achievements the future reputation of the school rested. There was a certain blind and archaic logic behind it all, although it raised a few questions which no grammar school was able to answer very satisfactorily. When the same division of labour was carried over into the comprehensive school in its early years, it posed a serious threat to staff relationships. Unless those in the most senior positions and earning the highest salaries were prepared to demonstrate their ability to handle the most difficult children, others were reluctant to take on the task. In that situation, mixed ability teaching had a certain appeal, since it manifestly put all teachers on the same footing. It is, however, important to realize that this part of the case for unstreamed classes has less to do with its efficacy as a means of teaching than with staff morale. It is in any case a less significant area of concern at the beginning of the eighties than it was twenty-five years ago. Comprehensive schools have now acquired specialist departments for working with the least able pupils, and those appointed to teach in them are not interested in having a share of the more academic cake. Added to that, a new kind of head of department has emerged who is able to work with children of all kinds and who insists on demonstrating his ability to do so. In a mature comprehensive, the staff might well feel insulted by any suggestion that there was jealousy over who took the clever children. Today, good staff relationships do not depend upon the absence of streaming and setting. If they did, it would be a sad comment on the teaching profession in the last quarter of the twentieth century.

The suggestion that unstreamed classes reduce discipline problems brings us back to that insoluble difficulty identified earlier – how to segregate without stigmatizing. Where a system of separating children of different abilities creates a group known as 'the Cs', discipline problems will inevitably arise. If mixed ability teaching had shown itself capable of overcoming that hazard, while at the same time meeting the needs of boys and girls of every potential, I would grapple it to me with bands of steel; but it has not. Very few unstreamed schools find it feasible to keep children of all abilities together for a common programme. Almost invariably, the least able are removed from some subjects that are beyond their competence or withdrawn from some lessons to be given special remedial help. Identification necessarily attends these arrangements. There is no way of meeting the needs of the extremely slow learner without letting everyone know who he is.

Unapologetic recognition of those with learning difficulties, and the creation of special programmes for them, is not only the best way of meeting their educational needs but also the best way of overcoming any idea that such children are inferior to the rest. The blinding truth is this: attempts to obscure the identity of the backward simply serve to reinforce wrong attitudes towards them. Openness is the key.

Whether or not identification leads to the great put-down for pupils who do not find the learning process a bed of roses depends on the style of provision made for them. The want of anything significant for 'the Cs', other than the label itself, affected all aspects of the life of Eltham Green School in 1970. In classrooms, corridors and playgrounds, the few made life miserable for the many and set an example that those of weak moral inclination were only too ready to follow. It was clear that disciplinary innovations had to be accompanied by important changes in the curriculum.

Money became available because of the imminent raising of the school leaving age. Most of it was invested in building and equipping two new specialist areas: a remedial wing and a social education wing. The first was to provide for children in the first three years of secondary education who had serious learning difficulties. The second was to meet the needs of those in the fourteen-to-sixteen age group described down the years as the unacademic, the early leavers, the Newsom group, and so on. Some of the labels tell us as much about ourselves as they do about boys and girls. Take that first one: the unacademic. I myself have no great confidence in the notion that, when our Creator made heaven and earth and all that therein is, he divided human beings into two kinds, the educable and non-educable. But there is no doubting that some teachers see perfectly ordinary children in that way. Unacademic youngsters are thought of as not really belonging in school at all. The sooner they are out of the education system, the better. Schools are for those who have a natural capacity for learning. While not denying that some children *would* be better off leaving earlier than they do, and strongly holding the view that the law should allow greater flexibility in that regard, it is not my experience that we need despair of educating what in some schools amounts to between ten and twenty per cent of the population. Through a social education programme, we hoped to show those who had rejected the education system – and who had been rejected by it – that they mattered as much as everyone else. But sadly that particular opinion is not sufficiently widespread in the typical English staffroom.

The remedial department was created by converting part of the main school building into a ten-classroom unit with each classroom able to accommodate up to fifteen pupils. A head of department and a team of seventeen teachers, six full-time and eleven part-time, now work in the remedial wing. Some are classroom teachers, while others specialize in the teaching of reading to individuals and small groups. After an initial investment allowing the team to acquire whatever equipment and materials they required, the department has continued to receive a very significant share of the school's annual resources. Of the £35,300 distributed to twenty departments in the academic year 1979-80, it received £1,100. This was about half the figure allocated to English and mathematics and about the same as that devoted to history and geography. The head of the department is one of the school's five Senior Teachers.

These few bare facts tell a story. The key to the success of remedial provision in any school is that it be seen as a *prestigious* activity. If the staff of a remedial department believe that what they are doing is important, and that it is so regarded by the leadership of the school, there will be a significant carry-over to the children placed in their care. Conversely, if remedial specialists have the poorest accommodation, the smallest allocation of resources and the leftovers of the responsibility posts, one should not be surprised if teachers and pupils become demoralized. Bearing in mind how big a part morale plays in working with slow learners, it is not surprising how little is achieved in certain situations. In one school the man in charge of a thoroughly inadequate remedial programme was officially designated the less able head of department. There is indeed a common belief in the teaching profession that those who work with remedial classes are somehow less intelligent than others. Nothing could be further from the truth, but it is a myth that will continue in circulation so long as head teachers declare their concern for the backward but fail to give adequate resources and status to those who teach them. It needs to be said that our colleges of education are not without fault in this matter. Only relatively recently have the needs of the slow learner received anything like adequate attention in secondary training courses, and there are still too few opportunities for specialization. In consequence, many remedial departments recruit from the primary sector. The National Foundation for Educational

Research is currently carrying out an investigation, due to be completed by the end of 1981, under the heading 'Provision for Slow Learners in the Secondary School'. One of its ten aims is to consider 'the role, status and training of the remedial specialist.' It is a subject that is long overdue for attention.

The remedial department at Eltham Green School provides for children in three categories. Firstly, the twenty pupils with the most serious learning problems on admission at eleven spend half their school week in the department, working for most of the time in classes of ten. Secondly, a further fifty pupils spend one-seventh of their week in the department, working together with the first group in classes of eleven or twelve. Thirdly, the teaching of reading is provided for all those pupils in the school whose reading age falls below ten. About three hundred pupils have reading lessons each week, these being arranged on a withdrawal basis.

This brief outline tells another story, or rather repeats one told before. Open identification of those in need is essential. So is open acknowledgement of their achievements. I linked first-year Angela's achievements to those of a sixth-former when I was speaking at a public function one year. Simon had scored four grade B passes at GCE A level, which was not bad and earned him some applause from the assembled company. But the warmest ovation was given to the little girl who entered the school at eleven with a reading age of seven and in just one year raised it to twelve, so that it matched her chronological age. When comprehensive schools feel free to be more open about their Angelas, we will know the day of the slow learner has truly arrived, and that he or she really does matter as much as the academically gifted.

After it had been established for six years, the remedial department published a report on its work. My own preface to the report contained these words:

> . . . the nature of our remedial organization requires open and acknowledged segregation of pupils. I once thought this to be an unfortunate necessity, thrust upon us by the overriding needs of

those for whom learning was a massive uphill struggle. But my view of this has changed significantly in recent years. I now believe it to be positively beneficial for children's weaknesses to be openly acknowledged, as their strengths have always been. To suggest, as some do, that we must not let it be known which children need special help because they will be denigrated by others is an appalling comment on the condition of our comprehensive schools. If we cannot teach children sympathy and understanding for those unlike themselves, what is the purpose of our comprehensiveness?

The same sentiments might have been expressed even more forcibly had I been writing about provision for the fourteen-to-sixteen age group. The creation of a social education department at Eltham Green was without doubt the most important single factor in the school's emergence in the seventies as one of the most heavily oversubscribed in the capital. Once the needs of the most disruptive element in the school population had been met, everything else followed almost as a matter of course.

The plan to set up an entirely separate social education wing with its own staff and curriculum was universally welcomed on both the academic and pastoral sides. It was indeed the only one of my initial proposals to have that kind of reception. That was not the result of any cleverness on my part in the way the scheme was put forward – it simply reflected the feeling almost of despair which was current at that time. Anyone who had some idea of what to do about the fourth-year heavy mob would have been welcomed as a sort of messiah. A programme that promised to take them off the hands of the ordinary classroom teacher was bound to be approved, for all the right reasons and for all the wrong reasons.

For all the right reasons, a huge number of applicants came forward when posts in the new department were advertised. There are a great many people in the teaching profession looking for an opportunity to work with disadvantaged teenagers, given the right conditions. Our social education wing was made up of a suite of classrooms flanking a large multi-purpose area which incorporated what we rather pretentiously called a coffee lounge when we had visitors round. Pupils belonging to the department were allowed to use this at break and during the lunch hour, the first of several privileges not shared by those taking more traditional courses. This privileged position would, of course, have achieved nothing and have been counter-productive had not two other factors applied. Firstly, the curriculum for those concerned was relevant to their situation. Secondly, they had to observe the same standards of dress and behaviour as others, despite belonging to what was very obviously a school within a school.

It was essential that pupils falling into the hands of our social educators should have examination opportunities. At first, some of the staff did not grasp this point, but it quickly became obvious. Noble notions of having done with the straitjacket of examination requirements quickly disappeared when it became clear that parents and pupils did not want to know about a course that excluded the possibility of Jimmy getting his certificate.

There were protracted negotiations with the CSE board when we submitted our mode three syllabus in social education for their consideration. They had not seen anything like our specimen examination paper before and rightly described it as a pioneer venture. Their readiness to give it sympathetic consideration for that very reason was greatly to their credit and demonstrated that examination boards can be more flexible than is generally believed. The kind of questions set raised a few eyebrows in our own staffroom.

> You are seen smoking at the bottom gate at the end of this examination. The main school has finished lessons and is going to dinner. What are the problems raised for everyone involved. Explain your answer from each person's point of view. What do you do? Why?

> A teacher has two fourth-year boys in front of him. One is white and the other is black. They have been fighting and the black lad

explains to the teacher: 'He said that I was a monkey and ought to go back to the jungle, so I hit him. Then he hit me back.' The white lad agrees with the story. Who was at fault, and in what way? How would you help them understand each other a little more if you were the teacher?

Tony is 22 and Jane is 20. They have recently married and have just had their first major row. They are refusing to speak to one another at the moment. They both go out to work to help save for a family in the future, and Jane came home an hour after Tony to find him watching television with his dishes from the evening meal unwashed, the breakfast dishes left in the sink and no meal prepared for her. During the row, Jane said that Tony was always doing this and that he should do his part in running the house. Tony said he was tired. How could you help Tony see Jane's point of view? How could you help Jane see Tony's point of view? What suggestions would you make to get them talking again?

The first two questions were very close to the daily experiences of the boys and girls concerned; the third raised issues they were familiar with through contact with married brothers and sisters. The thrust of the whole social education programme was in the direction of building upon a pupil's actual experience of life. To that end, community service was an important element, and this brought us into our most serious area of difficulty with the CSE board.

It was our intention to assess in some way the work boys and girls did while in attendance for part of their school week at local primary schools, old people's homes and day centres for the handicapped. It was hoped that 35 per cent of the marks for the examination would be derived from this community service element, these being made up of 5 per cent for a diary kept by each pupil, 15 per cent for a taped oral examination exploring what he or she had discovered from being in an adult role, and 15 per cent awarded by a supervising member of staff for actual performance and qualities of character revealed. The CSE panel dealing with the submission were disinclined to accept either that understanding of an adult role could be quantified or that qualities of personal character could be assessed. Since the thinking of our social educators in these matters was to some extent based upon the work of the Farmington Trust, its findings were submitted to those dealing with our proposals. In the end, the board agreed to accept that 25 per cent of the total marks for the examination should be allocated in the way we intended, on the basis of 5, 10 and 10 per cent for the three ingredients. Fifteen months after the original submission, a structure for the whole examination was agreed:

Written Paper	25 per cent
Community Service	25 per cent
Project	25 per cent
Continuous Assessment	25 per cent

It was a major concession for the CSE board to agree to a scheme which allocated only a quarter of the total marks to a formal written examination. But this was essential to our purpose, since one of the most acute handicaps suffered by many of the pupils was an inability to express in writing what they perfectly well understood in their minds.

Since these early adventures, mode three examination programmes have been established in other subjects, and there have been a great many developments of one kind or another in the social education programme. One of the most significant has been the introduction of a work experience scheme which takes the boys and girls out into the real world of work. In local supermarkets, department stores, factories and garages, they learn the truth about what awaits them. There have been some penetrating revelations in the reports and comments coming back. 'There was', said one husky young giant after a spell with the borough parks department, 'no playtime.' He was not the only one to discover a thing or two:

'I found it a bit hard to get up at the times *they* want.'

'It makes your legs ache.'

'I was told off for leaning against a wall and not *looking* busy.'

A works foreman summed up the situation: 'Work is such a shock to them.' We have certainly found some youngsters' passion for leaving school at the earliest opportunity significantly affected by a taste of work experience. A number of the girls have found it impossible to face, perhaps being less resigned than boys to the inevitability of working for a living for any length of time. There has not always been parental support. Mothers have withdrawn their children if they have been given menial tasks. Sometimes parents have as much to learn about the real world as their offspring.

The greatest problem with any work experience scheme, apart from the years of negotiation needed to set it up, is making sure everyone knows what it is for. Parents, pupils and those offering placements are all inclined to believe that, no matter what the school says, the object is for children to be found suitable employment ready for when they leave school.

My brief definition of social education when introducing it at the beginning of the seventies was unoriginal but to the point. It was not so much a programme, more a way of life. The analysis remains apt. Parents are still told that it is not a subject but a way of teaching subjects. The flexibility that is essential to the whole operation depends on staff and pupils being completely committed to it and having little or no involvement elsewhere in the school's organization. This enables the head of department to close down the timetable when he chooses and launch into short-run schemes without this affecting the normal running of the rest of the school. Once a year, a week is given to an exploration of the capital under the somewhat provocative title 'Let's Hit London'. In the summer term, a mock wedding at the local parish church provides a starting point for work on the home and family. The one hundred and fifty pupils taking the social education course are all involved. They dress up for the occasion, the ceremony is properly conducted by the vicar, and there is a reception back at school afterwards. Children from our feeder primary schools are also involved. One little girl's letter of thanks said, 'I liked the pretend wedding when Lorraine got married, but I saw her up Eltham after with another man.' On two occasions, members of the local community have written to say we shouldn't allow our pupils to get married so young.

It would be idle to pretend that there remains no element of stigma when a pupil is recommended for remedial support or advised to enter the social education department. But when such children are seen to be treated as if they matter and to be reaching for success and achieving it, there can be no basis for others to denigrate them. The wide variety of interesting activities in the social education programme is the envy of many children not recommended for consideration by the department. The problem today is not in persuading parents to let their first-year children enter the remedial department, but in getting them to agree when the time comes for a boy and girl to transfer to a normal course. 'Don't you dare move him out,' said one mother, 'he's never been so proud and happy in his life.' When pride becomes the mark of a child with learning problems, things are moving in the right direction.

Meeting the needs of 'the Cs', and relieving them of the burden of that label, was an important part of the answer to Eltham Green's disciplinary problems. There was another matter bearing closely upon the timetable and curriculum which also received early attention: the structure of the school day. The story of the changes that occurred provides an interesting illustration of how the disciplinary situation in a school bears upon academic decisions. Heads of departments were invited to consider changing from a seven-period day to a six-period day on the following grounds:

1   There was an urgent need to reduce movement about the school. A great many behaviour problems had their origin in the corridors and in the lifts between lessons.
2   Fewer changes of room, subject and teacher would be of particular benefit to children of least ability.
3   Teachers would face fewer pupils in one day.
4   The impact of staff absence would be less since classes would miss fewer lessons and face fewer strange teachers not qualified to teach the subject being covered.

5   An even number of periods in the day would make the construction, interpretation and operation of the timetable simpler.

This list represents a whole philosophy of school management. It says that the function of a school's organization is simply to establish those arrangements most likely to promote effective classroom teaching. The intention must be to bring together the teacher and his class in such a way that teaching may begin without delay and proceed to the greatest possible effect. If that seems a platitude, it is often ignored. Increasingly, one hears talk of the school day being organized so as to solve the everlasting problem of lunchtime supervision, come to terms with the failings of local transport, promote after school activities, and so on. Usually, one cannot have it both ways. When a school timetable becomes subject to some other consideration than how best to make classroom teaching effective, it ceases to perform its proper function.

There are already huge pressures on schools to give priority to activities that have little or nothing to do with the teaching process. The very fact of bringing a great many children together in one place five days a week makes it convenient to use the situation for all kinds of purposes. Within a week or two of being moved from primary to secondary school, boys and girls are pulled out of lessons for the medical people to find out what is in their hair, what is the state of their eyesight, what is happening to their teeth, their feet and various parts of the anatomy in between. Vaccinations and inoculations are annual staging posts, until the time comes for more of what one started with in the form of medical examinations before leaving. Meanwhile, lesson time has also been missed so that this class may complete a questionnaire for the inspectorate or that pupil be seen by the careers office. All of these things, and more besides, increasingly threaten to overwhelm the principal activity for which a school exists, namely classroom teaching. Of course, a great many of them must be done in the children's interests, and there is no denying that school is the most convenient place for them to be carried out. But it would be well to recognize the difficulty of convincing children that working hard at their lessons should take first priority when they are constantly being removed from them for some other purpose than teaching.

If the promotion of classroom teaching is the overriding concern in a school's organization, that is not to say that the structure selected should be allowed to become sacrosanct. After the first half of the seventies had passed, Eltham Green moved back to a seven-period day because conditions in the school had changed. Three of the five reasons for having six periods had become unimportant. Behaviour and movement about the school presented few difficulties; the children of least ability were no longer required to move from lesson to lesson but were based for a great deal of their time in the remedial department; staff absence was no longer a matter for concern. On the other hand, as teaching became more effective, pressures developed to broaden examination opportunities. Thirty periods in a week were not enough to accommodate all we wished to do for children of average and above average ability, so the seven-period day returned.

Sitting in the heads of departments meeting at which that decision was made, my mind went to the advice which John Colet, the founder of St. Paul's School, used to offer his staff and pupils: ever take a fresh, new, good purpose. A change of purpose will often rejuvenate an old idea and make it into a new one. What proves unthinkable today may well become the obvious course of action tomorrow when conditions change. One of the greatest dangers in running a school for any length of time is the inclination to believe you have seen it all before and that everything worthwhile has been tried already and either accepted or rejected. I once taught with a long-serving schoolmaster whose response to any suggestion for change was always, 'We tried that a long time ago and it didn't work.' I thought him very wise in the ways of the world, but now I realize it was not so.

There was a powerful temptation to stay with our six-period day, safe and secure within its confines. Some senior members of staff did not hesitate to seek its preservation by quoting at me just those arguments I had used when introducing it. But change was necessary, and not only in order to provide wider curricular opportunities for the most industrious and intelligent. In a really large school, change is a stimulant. Without it, the monster wallows. What Jacob Bronowski said about the ascent of man needs to be borne in mind by anyone running a school: 'Human achievement is not a museum of finished constructions. It is a progress.'

There was one other timetable innovation at the beginning of the seventies which has had a great influence on Eltham Green's journey since. It concerned all those children in the lower school who were not spending any classroom time in the remedial wing. A timetable was constructed which enabled departments to make their own decisions about whether to teach the great majority in ability groups or mixed ability groups (see Table 3).

The 390 pupils coming into the school were divided into two halves or populations, each covering the whole range of ability

Table 3: Teaching Groups, Autumn 1970

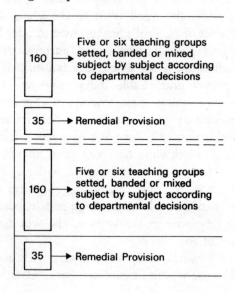

(the system described as parallel banding in the London notation illustrated in Table 1). In the group of 195 pupils which made up each half, 35 were identified as needing remedial provision within their timetables. The remaining 160 constituted the main stream and were timetabled together under five or six teachers in each subject. A head of department might choose to set this group finely; he might create a top set, a bottom set, and a middle ability band covering three sets; he could if he and his staff wished make five or six mixed ability groups. Interestingly enough, the English Department followed its yearning for the latter, but after a few years gave it up and turned to setting.

These arrangements derived from my conviction that teachers must be treated as professionals. The right people to choose how to teach English are the specialists in the field. Decisions about whether to set or mix in mathematics should be taken by those who actually do the job in the classroom, not by the headmaster or the inspectors or the governors or Her Majesty's Government. Again, there is nothing very original or startling in that belief, but it is currently under threat. There seem to be a great many people at some comfortable distance from the chalkface who consider themselves qualified to pronounce how teachers should teach. There is no area in which that is more true than in the streaming *versus* mixed ability debate. For myself, I feel totally unqualified to decide what my heads of departments should do. Of course, I have my own views about it, but the timetable structure says they must make up their own minds. It also enables me to say to visitors who ask whether we stream them or have mixed ability teaching, 'Yes, and everything in between.' Logic suggests that it is bound to be so, for who can say that one way is right for all subjects and for all teachers for all time? The great advantage of the style of parallel banding described is not only that it allows each department to go its own way, but it also permits a change of mind and of method as the years go by and one's academic chickens come home to roost.

For a few years there was one departure from the structure described above. As the school began to be oversubscribed and the proportion of children of high academic calibre increased, the director of studies and some heads of departments felt that special provision should be made for the brightest boys and girls. In the autumn of 1974, a top stream was introduced in the first year, made up of the 30 most able newcomers. They were taught as a group throughout their three years in the lower school, and the same procedure was followed with the intakes of 1975 and 1976. In 1977 it became necessary to create two such groups because of the steadily increasing number of bright children.

In 1978, two good reasons had emerged for abandoning the arrangement. Firstly, what had originally been seen in terms of one fast top stream of 30 pupils had developed into something much bigger. The yardstick we had used was the level of ability shown on a child's primary school transfer profile. At this time, the Inner London Education Authority put a primary school leaver into one of three ability groups in English, in mathematics and in verbal reasoning:

Group 1	Upper 25 per cent
Group 2	Middle 50 per cent
Group 3	Lower 25 per cent

We had been identifying our high-flyers as those earning a 1 in all three of the nominated areas of ability. In 1974 there were only 23 pupils designated 1.1.1. so there was no problem, the number 30 being made up by adding the best of those with just two top assessments. But by 1976 the total of new entrants bearing the distinction 1.1.1. had doubled, and there were also a great many youngsters with two top assessments who were clearly of very high academic ability. By 1977, 100 pupils were identified as of group 1 ability in verbal reasoning (another name for intelligence), the majority with a straight flush of top grades on their transfer documents.

But sheer numbers constituted only one reason for our abandonment of a fast top stream. More important was the development of wrong attitudes among the pupils concerned, and among some of the staff. Just as there had previously been the problem of 'the Cs', there now arose the problem of the high-flyers. Precocious in ability, they became the same in their behaviour. It was like being back in a grammar school again with boys who thought they were of greater value to the human race than most of their peers. It was a view encouraged by some teachers. An elegant girl (the clever ones usually are) was pulled up in the corridor for fooling about. A passing teacher had stopped to correct her: 'We don't expect that sort of thing from someone in your form. You're supposed to set an example to the rest.' Then turning to point to someone else who would never be elegant, clever, or out of trouble for long, and for all to hear: 'It would be different if it was *her.*' Elitism in a nutshell. It is the teaching profession which makes fast streams such a dangerous presence in a comprehensive school.

But that does not mean we ought not to identify those of high ability, separate them out if that provides the most effective teaching, and stretch them to their limit. As with those of least ability, the key to success is in the method of identification and the style of provision. Experience teaches me that subject ability setting is the least dangerous method of segregating clever children from the rest. It gives them fewer opportunities than streaming to acquire arrogant attitudes.

It is of some interest to examine the policies that departments in the school have adopted towards pupils in the main stream after a decade of being left to decide for themselves how to operate within the parallel banding structure.

English and Mathematics

Both departments test the children on entry and then set them into ability groups. The testing is done because the grades given on primary school transfer profiles have proved unreliable. We take children from upwards of thirty primary schools (it was 51 at one stage) and there is little consistency of assessment between them. While John Slow might be identified as of limited ability at Posh Street Primary, he could well be seen as average Grim Lane Junior. Attempts to moderate assessments centrally go some way towards establishing a common standard, but the results are less than exact at the margins of ability. When it comes to fine setting, it is necessary to make accurate marginal judgements, hence our tests. Since setting by subjects is by its very nature more precise than general streaming, there is no disguising the high degree of separation that has been instituted in English and mathematics.

Science
There is a top set in each half of the timetable. Below this there is banding of pupils of average ability into three or four parallel classes, each containing the same spectrum of ability.

Foreign Languages
There is one high ability set selected in each of the two languages taught. Below that level, French is taught in mixed ability groups while Spanish is setted.

History, Geography, Music, Drama and Religious Studies
These subjects practise a common policy. There is an upper band of sixty pupils of high ability in each half of the timetable, divided into two parallel classes of thirty. Pupils of average ability constitute a lower band, being divided into a number of parallel classes.

Design and Technology
Those with the best design potential are grouped together. The rest are in mixed ability groups.

Home Economics
There is mixed ability teaching.

Art
Pupils move between groups to acquire different skills.

Physical Education
There is mixed ability teaching.

The most common feature is the separation of pupils of high ability from the rest. The same applies, of course, to those of least ability, who are not included in this analysis of the main stream. The only group where there is no high degree of selectivity in most classroom subjects is the one in the middle which caters for those of average ability. But even here, although a number of departments claim to have mixed ability classes, the range is not wide since the extremes are not included. What has emerged as a result of the independent decisions of the various departments over a decade appears to be not all that different from the three ability bands which were dispensed with so decisively ten years ago. The French have an apt proverb: the more things change, the more they stay the same.

But it is an illusion. We have come a long way. While there are relatively few ways of teaching children, the beliefs and assumptions lying behind two apparently similar structures may be dramatically different. Two houses may look alike yet rest on very different foundations; and they may vary enormously on the inside. What is more, the outcome of any particular form or structure, the sort of life it makes possible, will be determined not only by the nature of the structure itself but also by its history. In the spring of 1976, Alexander Solzhenitzyn explained on British television his concern about what he called 'a people which no longer remembers'. If we forgot how we came to be where we are, we will lose track of our purpose.

One of the lessons to be learned is that it is the professional duty of teachers to be thinking all the time about what they are doing. Ask the next secondary teacher you come across about the composition of the classes he teaches. If he is typical, he will have no accurate idea of the ability range in some of them. All efforts to make proper and adequate provision for children of all abilities within a comprehensive structure will come to nought if teachers lose track of how systems have originated and how they are supposed to operate. Building an organization within which good teaching can take place is therefore only a beginning. One of the tasks of the head teacher is constantly to remind people what sort of structure they are in and how it came to be built.

When Basil Hume was the Abbott of Ampleforth and Headmaster of Ampleforth College, he had this to say when his role was examined in a television documentary: 'Leadership here means my seeing that the strong have something to strive for while the weak are never overwhelmed. There is therefore no question of people being treated equally.' Some would have us believe that the best way of organizing the teaching process is by pretending that all children are capable of much the same. But it is not so, and we go in that direction at our peril. The way out of difficulty at Eltham Green School was not to abandon the separation of one pupil from another but to recognize it more openly and to meet its implications head-on. It is no surprise or disservice to children to make known to them their differences from one another. They are aware of them. They know they are not all equally clever. Our task is to treat them as equally valuable. The timetable and curriculum in a comprehensive school must, like everything else about the place, say one thing above all others: everyone matters. Once that truth is encapsulated in a teaching structure, there remains the need constantly to remind classroom staff what lies behind the organization. It was once said of a most distinguished director of studies in a large comprehensive school that his timetable was a masterpiece but unfortunately he was the only one who understood it, as he was not much inclined to explain himself. It is reminiscent of what H. L. Mencken said of President Calvin Coolidge: 'He don't say much, and when he does, he don't say much.'

A great deal needs to be said, and to be repeated regularly, concerning the purpose of the academic structure adopted by a school. That is because, to return to the point with which this chapter began, a school's philosophy resides in its timetable and curriculum.

Four

Parents

The huge man who moved into my study behind the father of a boy in trouble elected not to take a seat when invited. Instead, he stood quietly by the door, available if needed. In reply to my inquiry, the parent explained: 'He minds me, don't he.' It was not a question but a simple statement of fact. Dealing with members of the criminal subculture this parent represented is a necessary part of running a comprehensive school. Those who make their living by breaking the law are just as likely as anyone else to have children and send them to school. It is not always easy to welcome the boy or girl who is being carefully trained to be a thief, but that is precisely what being comprehensive involves. On one occasion I was asked by a local shopkeeper, 'Why do you have all those nasty, foul-mouthed thugs at your school?' I told him, 'Because there are nasty, foul-mouthed adults who produce families, just like you and me.' I don't think he understood what I was talking about. His eyes said it was all the school's fault.

En route to Dover for a day trip to Boulogne, the school coach took a party of pupils through Canterbury. Hoping to awaken some interest in the cathedral, a teacher asked if anyone knew about the famous building in the city. Up shot Freddie's hand without hesitation or embarrassment. 'I know, miss. There's a nick. And me uncle Joe's in it.' It is not easy to bring home to such children the notion that criminal activity is something to be ashamed of. To regard the Freddies of this world as youngsters whose only hope lies in their being rescued is to ignore reality. They and their parents often understand their situation, and what has brought them to it, better than we think. There is little

51

or no prospect of changing their moral code or way of life. We have to educate them as best we can on the assumption that they will go on being what they are.

Fifteen-year-old Janice had run away from home and been picked up working on a street barrow in the Soho area. The owner of the barrow had provided her with bed and board in exchange for services rendered, some of which had been given outside what might be called normal business hours. By the time the police found her, Janice had dyed her hair red and inserted rings in her ears without having them properly pierced first. Impetigo was rapidly spreading all over her face, and the marks remain to this day. She sat with her mother in my study. 'Janice's been a bloody fool, ain't she?' said her mother. 'Well,' responded the girl, 'at least I got away from you lot.' Perhaps if our experience of adolescence had been living in two rooms with a boozy mother and seven younger brothers and sisters, sharing a toilet with two other families, we might be qualified to condemn her action and her attitude. Janice's pursuit of *la dolce vita* brought a change in the family circumstances by way of rehousing. While not inclined to encourage young people to revolt against their parents, that was one occasion when I found myself tempted to believe the ends had gone some way to justifying the means.

Jane's father arrived without an appointment, but he managed to see me all the same. His daughter was beyond our control and showed every sign of maladjustment. Father dropped himself into a chair in front of my desk and announced, 'I've come to tell you about our Janey, what's wrong wiv 'er.' He had the ease and confidence of a genuine working-class philosopher and would have done Drury Lane proud as Alfred Doolittle.

'We moved up 'ere, y'see, to your posh Eltham Park, from down in Bethnal Green. Down there, our Janey 'ad lots of friends, and most of 'em was 'er relations. Of a night, she'd be out in the street playin' wiv the uvver kids, or else we'd know she was down a few doors at auntie's or up a few at me sisters or maybe down the end wiv 'er cousins. But what 'appens now, in your posh Eltham Park? She ain't got no friends or relations to play wiv. The kids there, y'see, they don't play out. Where are they? I'll tell you where they are, 'eadmaster. They're locked up in their bleedin' conservatoires, playin' their bleedin' violins.'

Jane's father had put his finger precisely on the problem created for a child by the breakdown of the old street community which was once a feature of London life. Down in Bethnal Green, the local street was a caring organization where everyone looked after everyone else and where the extended family stretched from one end of the road to the other. They were their own social workers and welfare officers – and probably their own educational psychologists too. They belonged together and they knew it. The isolation of the middle-class suburban lifestyle – something which those born to it find difficult enough to face – had destroyed Jane's sense of belonging to the community in which she lived. The teacher's art of listening is something to be exercised not only in the classroom. Letting parents talk is one of the quickest routes to the truth, for often they are wiser in the ways of their children than we are. Our Janey's dad was a reminder of that.

The parents who worry me most are the members of the intelligentsia who say things like, 'I am sending my son to a comprehensive school because my philosophy of education tells me that is what I should do.' I am not too happy about parents who use their children to realize their own philosophical obsessions. I would much rather hear someone say he is sending me his youngster because he thinks we will 'learn him proper'. But coming to terms with the ideas and aspirations of articulate parents with clever children is an important duty laid upon a comprehensive school. It is one which leads into difficult territory. Sometimes, emphasis on achieving good academic results with the brightest children takes too great a priority. At the other extreme, resistance to the well-informed parent can become an automatic reaction.

The greatest mistake made in the early years of comprehensive education in this country was the attempt to emulate grammar school priorities, traditions and emphases. It was understandable, since public confidence was seen to depend upon the ability of the new organization to achieve academic success with the brightest children as effectively as the system it was replacing. It was for this reason that the headships of the most extravagantly built comprehensives tended to go to teachers from grammar schools. Very few of the most prestigious new buildings were placed in the hands of people coming from the secondary modern sector. This said a good deal about what local authorities, school governors, inspectors and the rest thought the business of running a school was about. Success was seen in terms of what the grammar schools had achieved with the top twenty per cent of the child population. It is an idea that persists, and it is in danger of receiving fresh life from the growing concern about standards. Inevitably, the voices raised most loudly tend to be those of parents with clever children. But if our anxious glances look only in that direction, we do a great disservice to eighty per cent of the next generation of adults. If the comprehensive school stands for anything at all, it is for stretching every sort and condition of child to the limit of his abilities. That was often said in the forties and fifties when the new system had its genesis, but there was precious little evidence in some quarters that anyone really believed it. The lion's share of resources and interest went to the children whose performance was destined to show that grammar school achievements could be reproduced in a comprehensive setting. It has taken a quarter of a century for the injustice and unwisdom of that to become plain. The early history of the comprehensive school sometimes looks very much like an educational confidence trick. We must not revert to previous bad practice because of political and public anxiety about standards. The world has moved on, and today's uneasiness, which is not by any means unwarranted, should embrace the whole spectrum of boys and girls. If the debate about children reaching benchmarks of competence focuses only on what the cleverest children achieve and what a school's GCE results are, we shall be back where we were before in the world of the neglected eighty per cent.

That is not to say we do not owe it to the parents of the most able children to give as much attention to their boys and girls as the rest. It is no more excusable to leave the best young scientific minds in the country to make the most of it in a mixed ability physics group than it is to give them all the attention and applause. 'Neglect none' would be a good motto for a comprehensive school; but it is an intention not easily realized. 'Reject none' would also be suitable, but some parents invite rebuff. There is nothing so difficult for a school as welcoming the criticism of an informed, professional parent who speaks the educational lingo and is able at a glance to discern the difference between what one claims to be doing and the reality. 'I suppose', said a perceptive mother, 'you have been forced into this by the shortage of maths teachers?' How dare she discover so readily the real reason for what we called a redeployment of time between subjects! No wonder teachers become paranoic.

Doubtless schools should be more open about what they are doing. If parents have faith in a school and its leadership, they will accept almost anything one says to them. But it is not always easy to explain things in terms which can be properly grasped. Often it is only the erudite minority who really understand, and they are well able to work it out for themselves anyway. A good illustration is provided by the debate about examination results. There is a commonly held belief that publication of results presents no problems of interpretation provided a school's performance is related to the quality of its intake. Although myself very much in favour of making results known, I am convinced that telling the whole truth in a way people are able to understand is not nearly as simple as some suppose. Educational statistics alone mean little to the average parent and not very much to the average teacher. The innumeracy among children which worries us so much is pretty widespread in the adult population too. 'Don't show me any of your numbers,' said a father who knew his limitations, 'tell me how some of them got on at A level.' That sort of request brings a sigh of relief to the head teacher, who is always a master at the art of making the most of his best individual results. And therein lies the nature of the problem. Since statistics alone are so often meaningless, they have to be interpreted. What is made of them depends always on the interpreter. Every year as the leaves turn to gold, head teachers declare their examination results with a glow of pride which matches the autumn tints. Astonishingly, every school is able at its annual prizegiving to report more and better passes than last year. Although teachers regularly complain that children are less industrious than they once were; that they move from primary to secondary school with lower standards of literacy and numeracy; that discipline is more difficult to maintain; that educational cutbacks make the whole job more and more impossible, yet it seems none of this is ever reflected in any school's examination performance. Which simply goes to show that we have learned to make the most of our achievements, be they few or many. That is not surprising, since schools exist in a highly competitive situation and many will be fighting for survival throughout the eighties. There are those, too, who interpret things to mean whatever they want them to mean. It will ever be so, and the publication of statistics will not solve the problem. The natural wish of parents to understand what is going on in a school will be satisfied to no significant degree by such data.

It is perhaps worthwhile to look fairly closely at the ordinary, average parent who has a child of moderate ability. What is such a person like at this stage in the evolution of our education system?

The average parent is for discipline; school uniform; plenty of homework; the right to choose a school and to have the choice honoured; high levels of professional competence and conduct on the part of teachers; having access to the head teacher. The ordinary mother or father is against mixed ability teaching; informality between teacher and taught; getting involved in school government; the public transport system which conveys children to and from school (or more likely fails to do so). He or she is suspicious of modern maths; the influence of local politicians and educational administrators; sex education. The middle-of-the-road parent is not sure about large schools; mixed schools (fathers of daughters are especially doubtful); what inspectors are supposed to do; how the public examination system works. Finally, most of those trying to bring up adolescent children at this time are apprehensive about employment prospects for their youngsters when they leave school.

Ordinary parents know and accept the truth of Virgil's words *sunt lacrimae reum*, there are tears in life. Raising children is no easy task and cannot be done without a good deal of anguish. Some of the advice offered over the years has not been all that helpful. That provided by Dr Benjamin Spock in his *Baby and Child Care* led many to allow their children a remarkably free hand in the fifties and sixties. In his 1974 sequel, entitled *Bringing Up Children in a Difficult Time*, he disclaimed responsibility for the way two generations of parents had interpreted his philosophy. 'How', he asked, 'did I ever get the reputation among some people of being an advocate of excessive permissiveness?' It is perhaps surprising that it took him nearly thirty years to raise that question. There are those who believe this would not be such a difficult time for bringing up children if he had done so before.

But there has never been an easy time for bringing up children. The words of Peter the Hermit, written shortly after the Battle of Hastings, strike an echo.

> The world is passing through troubled times. Young people today think of nothing but themselves. They have no reverence for parents or old people. They are impatient of all restraint. They talk as if they alone know everything and what passes for wisdom in us is foolishness to them. As for the girls, they are forward, immodest and unworthy in speech, behaviour and dress.

The difficulty for most parents lies in striking the right balance between accepting the inevitable need of the younger generation to reject outdated traditions and insisting on the preservation of those values that really matter. As in so many areas of life, the problem is where to draw the line. What *are* the standards for which parents should fight tooth and nail (and let's not pretend it doesn't come to that in some perfectly normal families)? What differentiates the second half of the twentieth century from what has gone before is that the answer to such a question is no longer readily available – not from those who govern us, not from the church, and certainly not from the communications media.

'I've tried to be a good parent,' said the father of a fifth-form boy who was in trouble, 'but I find it hard to know what's right and what's wrong these days. Everybody tells you something different.' He was not at all like the father depicted in John Osborne's *Look Back in Anger*: an old plant left over from the Edwardian wilderness who couldn't understand why the sun wasn't shining any more. In my own youth, that play was a magnificent revelation, a genuinely important experience. But its message is not for the eighties. My bewildered parent had few preconceived notions. He accepted that standards had changed and simply wanted someone to tell him with some kind of authority which ones continued to apply. It is common enough for teachers to assert that children need a structure within which to operate; one sometimes overlooks the fact that parents need the same. Without it, they become as lost as their offspring. In my experience, one of the duties the head teacher frequently has to take upon himself is to instruct parents in what they should and should not allow their children to get away with. This was the course I took with the parent in question. 'Thanks,' he said, 'now I know what to do.' But he added as an afterthought, 'Mind you, it's your fault if he leaves home.'

Thus do we find responsibility thrust upon us. It reminded me of an occasion during my time in a Liverpool comprehensive when a mother came to complain she hadn't been told that her boy had run away from home. She couldn't be expected to notice herself, seeing that she had two jobs and only saw him at weekends. The police had turned up with him one day and she hadn't even known he'd been away. It was right diabolical we hadn't told her. If she ever got asked about her most embarrassing experience, she was going to tell them about how our rotten school landed her in it. It was a sad, amusing incident which served to underline the extent to which parents are prepared to look to school for help, for support and for someone to blame. The head teacher must be prepared to say, somewhat like the prophet Isaiah: 'Here am I, blame me.'

Despite what has been said about the things of which the ordinary parent approves and disapproves, attitudes towards a school are not in the end determined by details of organization. It is the feel of an institution – what Professor Michael Rutter calls its ethos – which tells people whether or not to place their confidence and their children in it. It may be observed in the way the children move about and in the words and looks they exchange with one another and with their teachers. The impact of a school cannot be reduced to an account of its organizational features; it is as much in the emotions as in the mind. That is something which must be borne in mind when schools deal with parents. We should not be too concerned about offering careful expositions of school policy. The anxious mother or father sometimes wants no more than for a school to express confidence in itself. Effective leadership depends on faith in the person rather than the programme. The first disciples had some grave doubts about what Jesus was up to, but they followed the man. In the school setting, parents will place their faith in a good teacher without necessarily having any understanding of what he is doing. Interestingly, it is often the weak teachers who have to resort at parents' evenings to giving an account of their methods. Schools must, of course, be prepared to give straight answers to questions. But, as any doctor will tell you, what someone asks is not always what he wants to know. What the ordinary parent wishes to be assured of from time to time is that those who teach his children believe in what they are doing, no matter whether it can be explained in terms he understands.

There are two principal ways in which parents can take an active part in the general life of a school: through the PTA and by serving as governors. Neither evokes a great deal of enthusiasm at secondary level. Most parents are profoundly interested in the education of their own children, and are prepared to sacrifice their time in order to come to parents' evenings and similar occasions when work and progress are under review. They will stay for hours in a conscientious effort to see every teacher who takes their offspring and will make all kinds of sacrifices.

A similar level of commitment is rarely found when it comes to general activities. Most PTAs depend heavily upon the efforts of a relatively small group of people who find that social events are much better supported than educational ones. Whatever the degree of public anxiety about modern teaching methods, it has not yet reached such a dramatic pitch as to fetch many away from their television sets to an evening meeting on the subject.

The existence of a PTA presents two problems which are matched by two benefits. Some teachers have an innate suspicion of parents which is increased when they form what appears to be a power-group with special access to the head teacher. Some parents see a PTA as a means of bringing pressure to bear with regard to school policies. Neither problem is difficult to overcome if the head teacher is prepared to be closely involved in PTA affairs. Those schools in which such bodies get out of hand are ones where they are left to go their own way. The advantages of PTA activity are worth the risks. Giving parents opportunities to do something for the school at large, rather than just for their own children, cannot but generate a sense of unity and inter-dependence. PTA activities bring together all sorts and conditions of people and help them to understand and tolerate one another. Is it not reasonable to assume that, if parents of all kinds can learn to work as one, it may help their offspring to do the same? The second advantage of having a PTA did not occur to me when ours was first established at Eltham Green in 1971. It has come to be of almost overriding importance. Through the informal exchanges which take place at meetings, I discover what are the big issues in the minds of parents at any one time and what are the questions most worrying them. In a very large school, it is not easy for parents to make known their day-to-day anxieties. The PTA provides one means of finding out.

Very few parents are interested in taking part in the election of parent-governors, let alone serving on governing bodies. The voting figures for the elections in the seventies at Eltham Green

School are revealing, given that between a thousand and fifteen hundred parents were entitled to take part each time. They are similar to those for other schools.

Table 4: Voting Figures at Eltham Green School

Year	Number voting	Number of candidates	Votes cast for successful candidate(s)
October 1971	129	3	58
January 1972*	21	2	14
October 1972*	55	4	27
October 1973	60	1	60
September 1977	82	9	38
			35 } three seats
*By-election			35

No expense was spared to encourage parental involvement in the elections. Disappointed by the level of interest shown the first time in 1971, the Inner London Education Authority invested considerable resources in an attempt to rouse parents to a higher degree of involvement in 1973. A leaflet was printed at no small expense setting out the duties of a governor; a television programme was produced for showing in schools; an advertising campaign was conducted in local newspapers throughout London for a fortnight; schools were advised to send invitations to election meetings by post. The total financial cost of the exercise was never stated. The result in terms of parental interest was negligible.

The débâcle of parent-governor elections has made it unarguably clear that the great majority of parents have little desire to become involved in the running of schools. However, that does not mean it is not a good thing that greatness has been thrust upon them. The three parents who govern my school, together with the two teachers, are infinitely better qualified to do it than the dozen or more political nominees. It is those with a stake in a school who should have the strongest voice in how it is run, not those with the biggest political axe to grind.

The unacceptable face of parent power shows itself when those elected to govern schools are unrepresentative of the ordinary mother and father. Individuals with special knowledge and qualifications are rarely reluctant to step forward. Inarticulate parents feel inadequate and are inclined to vote for those who know all about education. The result is exactly the opposite of that most desired. There is no shortage of experts telling schools what to do. It is the voice of the average parent we need to hear — the one who leans forward quietly in the middle of a debate about creative English and asks how we teach children to spell. Give me governors about me who are ordinary.

Later in this book there is a chapter largely devoted to the government of schools and these issues will be taken up again there. At this stage, it simply needs to be emphasized that there *is* an important job to be done by parents in the field of school government. As the attempt is made in the eighties to take political control of schools through governing bodies, it will become ever more essential that those with a genuine interest in the particular children who go to make up a school at a given time should be watching over their interests.

In some human activities it is difficult to discern the chief influence at work, but this is not the case where the development of children is concerned. Without a shadow of doubt, power lies in the home. Boys and girls who succeed at school are those whose parents show continuing interest and concern, and who work hard at that most difficult exercise we call marriage. Invariably, a child's failure has its origin in the domestic situation. I have never come across a youngster with really serious problems in school that didn't arise from a situation at home. All things are possible in school if there is security at home. Conversely, very little is possible if all is not well in that most important of places. It follows that strengthening the home would be a sure way of strengthening the education system. When Dr Coggan, then Archbishop of Canterbury, proposed in the House of Lords on 16 June 1976 that the government should appoint a Minister for the Family, he knew what he was doing.

In the course of his speech, he read to their lordships an essay written by an eight-year-old boy on the subject of grandmothers:

> A grandmother is a lady who has no children of her own, so she likes other people's little girls and boys. A grandfather is a man grandmother. He goes for walks with the boys and they talk about fishing and tractors. Grandmothers don't have to do anything but be there. They are old, so they shouldn't play hard or run. Usually they are fat, but not too fat to tie children's shoes. They wear glasses and funny underwear, and they can take their teeth and gums off. They don't have to be smart, only answer questions like why dogs hate cats and why God isn't married. They don't talk baby-talk like visitors. When they read to us, they don't skip bits or mind if it is the same story over again. Everybody should have one, especially if they don't have television, because grandmothers are the only grown-ups who have time.

When parents fail to have time for their children, they damage them. Whatever the economic pressures, the need for someone to be there when Debbie gets home does not grow less. For her to be able to unload the day's troubles in that first few minutes, get a comforting pat and a biscuit and disappear into some corner with her copy of *Fabulous* while the tea is made, is more important than some parents realize. And it remains important all the way through school. If some sixteen-year-olds in my experience had been able to go home to somebody rather than nobody, their lives would have been a very different story. Of course, most children are able to cope with coming home to an empty house. But leaving children to cope is not the ideal. In *Mother Knows Best*, Dorothy Scannell describes her upbringing in the East End of London in the twenties like this:

> None of us walked down the grove on the way home from school. Some of us looked like competitors in a walking race all disqualified at the tape, for the magnetic pull of home was too strong for any of us to walk there . . . we would start to call, 'Mum', as soon as we turned into the gate. We leapt down the

steps to the kitchen and mother was always standing by the door in her black frock, lace collar pinned with a brooch which had an amber stone in the centre. The white cloth was on the table, the kettle singing on the fire, we were home.

The writer of that would smile at the suggestion that mothers today have no alternative but to go out to work to make ends meet. Her father was a plumber earning two pounds a week, on which princely sum ten children were raised. Yet their home was 'a happy place of roaring laughter'.

Such homes produce children who succeed at school, whatever their capabilities. A teacher's achievements are never entirely his own. Parents hold the key to educational success.

Five

Teachers

Talking of the student demonstrations in Europe and America in the sixties, the American writer and broadcaster Eric Sevareid described the attitude of the most extreme elements in unambiguous terms: 'We are right, they say. We are progress. If you resist us, or defend yourself, you are the instigators of violence.' (Quoted by Theodore White, *The Making of the President 1968*). There was a feeling among young people in places of higher education that their moment had come. Paradoxically where it was at its strongest, the actual teaching process came to a halt. The alternative society seemed to have no place for it.

Delivering the 1972 Dimbleby Lecture, Lord Annan talked about students' rights: a subject which still caused a good deal of excitement, although the hysteria of the sixties was over. He pointed out that the most important right of a student was to be well taught. It is a truth which bears upon and answers all kinds of questions which arise in places where education is carried on.

For example, it tells us what view to take of rewards and punishments. It has been suggested that schools spend too much time punishing children and not enough rewarding them. In effect, that is simply a comment on standards of classroom teaching. If a class is well taught, the attentive and industrious children will score good marks and earn favourable reports. The average youngster needs no more to motivate him. Special accolades are only necessary when the child who is doing his best fails to have that fact recognized in the course of normal lessons. It usually happens when an inadequate teacher has to spend all his time dealing with a few miscreants. Thus it is that bad teaching creates the need for both special rewards and extensive punishments. Good teaching is a reward in itself; being denied it, by being put outside when he knows it is going on, is punishment enough for the average child.

A year after Lord Annan's pronouncement, a sixth-form conference at Eltham Green School took education as its theme and considered the characteristics of a good teacher. Since delegates came from near and far, and since each had experienced more than ten years of schooling, their definition might be thought worth considering:

> The ideal teacher needs patience, humour, charisma, foresight, communication, tolerance, empathy, discipline, enthusiasm, saintliness, love and understanding.

Such a description almost brings discussion to an end, not to mention teacher recruitment. But if one accepts that reality may be permitted to fall a little short of the ideal, what are the most important of the qualities mentioned? Few would disagree if one identified the last two: love and understanding. A conversation between a sixth-former and a teacher a few weeks after the conference took this form:

> Sixth Form Girl: I wouldn't want to teach secondary. I don't know how you put up with them. How do you put up with them?
>
> Teacher: You have to love them. Whatever they do, you have to love them.

The teacher had been in the classroom too long to be a sentimentalist, and he added, 'Mind you, that doesn't mean you always have to like them.' It is an important distinction which has to be learned. The greatest teacher of all time showed us the way, as John Donne reveals: *'In finem dilexit eos*, saith Saint John. He loved them to the end. Not for any particular end, not for any use of his own, but to their end.' Endlessly caring, come what may, for children whose attitudes fill one with disgust is a task beyond the emotional reach of some who find their way into the profession. But the inability to take pleasure in teaching the utterly unlovely and thoroughly objectionable child disqualifies a teacher from regarding himself as a fully equipped and properly adjusted member of a state comprehensive system. That is not to say there are not still corners available for those who are able to work only with children who have a natural appetite and aptitude for true learning and good behaviour, but they are becoming fewer.

Concern for the least able and least motivated is an acquired talent. It takes years for a teacher to find out the whole truth about how children's minds work, especially those who at first appear to have no minds to explore. Anyone who thinks it is a matter of either understanding or not understanding boys and girls right from the start has it all wrong. Even for some parents, getting to the bottom of their children never goes beyond changing their nappies in babyhood. Teachers who claim to know all about those they teach after a term or two assume too much. And nothing could be less in the interest of the problem pupil than to be given what looks like understanding by someone who has none. The great test for a teacher handling a fourteen-year-old who has given up the search for a worthwhile life is to be able to wait for the truth to emerge. There are those in the profession and in the support services who fall foul of the temptation which came to Thomas Becket in *Murder in the Cathedral*:

> This last temptation is the greatest treason:
> To do the right deed for the wrong reason.

Infinite love and understanding do not come automatically to many teachers, except with a relatively narrow range of pupils whose experience of life is close to their own. Are there some more modest qualities which one may use as a yardstick for teaching in a comprehensive school? What does one look for when interviewing young probationers? There are some qualities all head teachers would agree about; there are others on which they would be divided. Five seem to fall into the first category.

COMMAND OF SUBJECT

No one can teach effectively in a comprehensive school who does not have a genuine command of his subject in the very broadest sense. Academic knowledge is not enough. There must be the ability to present it in different ways to children of different abilities. It requires a far higher degree of skill than that practised by the grammar school teacher working with clever children. It is one of the trademarks of a good teacher that he is able to make his meaning clear in simple terms which are understandable to those whose competence is far less than his own. At university level, it often distinguishes the professor who has a real grasp of his material from the young lecturer who is still finding his way. The person with a rich and mature acquaintance with his sources will be the one to produce just the right illustration to make all things clear. His students will say to themselves, 'Of course, it's obvious. Why couldn't I see that before?'

The ability to make the profound simple generally comes with age and experience. But that is not the whole story. Some teachers have the gift and some do not. Discerning whether or not a newcomer to the teaching profession will, in due course, be able to put over his subject to children of all kinds is not always easy. Those who are going to be bad at it are immediately obvious. They are the ones who have never really thought about the implications of working in a comprehensive setting. I once interviewed a history graduate who wanted children to see themselves in a world perspective. Asked how he would bring twelve-year-old children who could not read to such a view, he explained that he would write the notes on the blackboard in capital letters. He reminded me of a distinguished member of the faculty of psychology at one of our universities with whom I once shared a railway carriage following a public debate in which we had both taken part. 'You run one of these large comprehensive schools,' he said to me. 'Tell me, what on earth do you do with the kids who are only capable of one A level?' The existence of boys and girls unable to cope with one O level was something that had never occurred to him.

Such exchanges have to do with issues that are wider than a person's command of his subject. What that young historian lacked was an understanding of children. There are many teachers in comprehensive schools who started out with his conception of things and who in due course learned the truth; but some have been quite unable to bring their practice into line with their understanding.

It is not difficult to recognize the teacher who is going to be outstanding at communicating his subject at all levels. His ability to convey information in an illuminating way will quickly show itself in an interview, where one looks for a certain sense of inadequacy combined with an enthusiasm for getting it right. I remember one such interview.

Headmaster: Why do you want to teach science in a comprehensive school?

Candidate: I'm hoping to come across some children who are interested in it.

Headmaster: What about those who aren't? We've got plenty of them.

Candidate: I expect I shall be hopeless with them at first, but I'm sure I can make a go of it if you give me the chance.

The determined young woman who had that conversation with me now has a senior post at another comprehensive school. She is particularly good at advising young probationers, who find it a great comfort to be told, 'If you think you've got problems, you should have seen me when I started.'

Of course there are teachers to whom this generalization about the need to communicate at all levels of ability does not apply. Clearly, remedial specialists do not require it; nor do those coaching Oxbridge candidates in their seventh term in the sixth form. But at least three-quarters of the staff of any comprehensive must be able to teach across a fairly wide ability range. And falling rolls in the eighties will make it necessary for them to be able to do it in more than one subject.

RELIABILITY

In any kind of school, the unreliable teacher is a constant irritation. He is the one who never gets mark lists in on time; is dilatory about completing reports, and writes that Sally has had a good term when she has been away all the time; never arrives on time for break duty or for examination invigilation; cannot remember which material he has covered with which class. In a large comprehensive school, such people are a disaster, because they often remain undetected a good deal of the time and are not found out until it is too late for them to reform. Such people are often the ones who are most frequently absent. I had this to say on the subject in the *Weekly Educational Review* in the summer of 1979:

Quite a lot of pupils don't turn up these days. But truancy is not limited to children. Teachers are not as conscientious about attendance as they used to be. I have no national statistics to support that view, but would rest upon the wisdom of that great modern philosopher Muhammad Ali who said, 'I don't always know what I'm talking about, but I know I'm right.' I know I'm right when I say that regular, uninterrupted attendance at a school by all of its teachers is less general than once it was. The growth of the big unit partly explains this. In the old days (if you will pardon the expression) when schools had one or two or three dozen teachers in them, you knew which people would have to take your lessons if you were away. What was more, they knew you. But in a school with more than a hundred teachers, individual absences become an anonymous thing – and the human conscience does not operate very effectively in anonymous situations.

I quote that because of the aftermath: one of my most unreliable teachers accused me of unprofessional conduct in writing it.

The least professional teachers are absurdly sensitive about the need for others to be professional. The weaknesses I described are all forms of unprofessional conduct, in that they throw extra burdens on one's colleagues. Because I believe that, I have always had my really big rows with staff in the common room where everyone else may witness them. I clearly recollect the first of them. A young teacher was having a conversation there one morning when he should have been registering his form. I reminded him that his pupils were upstairs waiting for him, unsupervised. He blandly assured me that he would hear them if they got out of hand. In fact, he was depending on the teacher next door to sort things out should that happen. He was relying on the presence of a colleague who took a teacher's responsibilities more seriously than he did himself. There were witnesses who felt the offender should have been torn to pieces privately in my study rather than publicly in the common room. But it is the duty of a head teacher not only to make sure justice is done but also to allow others to see that it is done. I suspect the conscientious teacher derives some pleasure from seeing the slacker get his deserts.

In appointing staff at probationer level, it is usually easy to identify those with a low reliability rating because they are described in appropriate terms in college reports. But one has to be careful: once a student has been allowed to complete a course, colleges often feel honour-bound to present them without their warts. Some of those working in the field of teacher training take an extraordinarily sanguine view of the sort of people who should be admitted to the profession. As a teaching practice examiner in design and technology, I was astonished when a college lecturer with overall examining responsibility suggested that a candidate should be awarded a pass despite unarguable evidence that he had copied his dissertation from someone else's work. It was felt that, since he had succeeded in everything else, it would be a pity to keep him from the classroom and workshop because of one weakness!

A student teacher arrived at school one day looking like a tramp. After sending him back where he came from, we received a congratulatory telephone call from the college. It was time schools took some action about slovenly students. We were supposed to feel flattered, but my response was an angry one. On what basis did a college allow itself to send such people to stand in front of children in classrooms? Well, it was all very difficult, what with students' rights and all that sort of thing. It was pitiful. In case it be thought this has nothing to do with a teacher being professionally reliable, let me say the opposite is the case in my experience. Those students who do schools the courtesy of dressing properly, usually have high standards in everything else as well. Those who don't care what they look like, are ignorant of how the teaching process works. If we want children to aim high in their work and behaviour, we have to show them that everything about us is the best it can be. We teach by what we are; we are each our own visual aid.

SENSE OF HUMOUR

If ever there was an occupation in which it pays not to take oneself too seriously, teaching is it. This is because such a large proportion of what we attempt is destined to founder either on the rock of our own incompetence or on the shoals of our pupils' apathy. For we undertake an impossible task when we set out to interest and educate pupils of all ages and abilities in forty-minute sessions five or six times a day every week. Does an actor attempt more than one effective performance in twenty-four hours? Most days he does not; and even if his time on stage does run beyond forty minutes, his audience does not keep changing. Which leads me to the conclusion that a teacher should not expect to deliver more than half a dozen good lessons a week. Francois Truffaut, the French film director, has some apposite words to offer:

> Making a film is like making a journey in a wild west stage coach. At first you look forward to a good trip. Later you just

hope you will make it. You start out hoping to make the best picture of your life. In the end you are thankful if you manage to finish it.

What teacher has not had that experience in the classroom? We go in saying to ourselves, 'This is it. This is the big one. I've prepared a great lesson here.' Twenty minutes later, we are surreptitiously eyeing the clock, hoping we will survive.

There is another reason why a teacher must have a sense of humour: it finds a response in children. A teacher who cannot laugh with his class has not established the right relationship with them. The critical skill lies in being able to allow freedom while retaining control. The experienced professional makes it look easy, but it is not. Until that skill is acquired, a teacher is short of something he needs to have. It is especially important in dealing with the most difficult children – those whose experience of education has been all gloom and depression, and whose normal idea of a good laugh is to put a stop to whatever the teacher is trying to do. Converting humour into a constructive rather than a destructive force is what the sociologists call a fulfilling exercise. There is no question it can be done. The social education department at Eltham Green School, where our most problematic pupils are to be found, is full of the right kind of laughter. It is the sort you get in a family, where everybody knows the joke before anyone utters it. It is the product of closeness and caring.

LIKING FOR THE COMPANY OF CHILDREN

Almost the most important quality a teacher needs to have (the most important of all is being saved to last) is a liking for the company of children. Sadly, not all teachers possess it. Some manifestly dislike being with boys and girls and avoid it at every possible opportunity. Like the master of Dotheboys Hall, they view children as their proper and natural enemies. On the other hand, there are those who never tire of being with their pupils and who, not content with thirty lessons a week and every lunch hour and afternoon given over to out-of-school activities, take them off camping, canoeing or climbing at weekends and during the holidays. There is within the teaching profession a vast spectrum of attitudes towards spending time with children.

The same applies to parents. In the summer of 1979, the Council of Local Education Authorities came up with a suggestion for reducing winter fuel consumption. It was that English schools should adopt the continental school day, beginning early in the morning and finishing at lunch time. There were howls of protest from some parents. 'It's bad enough,' said one to a national newspaper, 'finding something to keep the kids occupied during the school holidays without having them home every afternoon.' Said another, 'It would be hell. It would drive me mad.' One wonders how people survived the rigours of parenthood before compulsory education provided a service for taking their children off their hands.

Seeing how unattractive some teachers find children to be, it is a mystery how they came to enter a profession that thrusts them into their company. This is something the teacher-training establishments ought to think about. One frequently wonders about their selection procedures. Having been involved in them myself on behalf of one college, I am inclined to think too much attention is given to subject specialization and not enough to suitability for teaching. This is no doubt in part due to the departmental structure of the institutions. Heads of academic departments are principally interested in the candidate with good A level results who might stay for four years and shed a little glory upon the laboratories or history wing in the form of an honours degree. Since that might even help a department to survive in the face of contracting student numbers, there is all the more reason to take a disproportionate interest in likely subject performance rather than teaching potential. The pressure on colleges to become third-rank university-type establishments is immense, and it has distracted them from what should be their first concern, namely finding and training people who enjoy the company of children and who will make good teachers.

It is not difficult to determine at an interview the extent of a teacher's commitment to being with children. One of the training tasks of a school is to see to it that the enthusiasm of the promising young teacher does not end in disillusion when the cynics get to work in the staffroom and the heavy brigade flexes its muscles in the classroom.

ACCEPTANCE OF STYLE

The first priority in appointing a teacher to a school is to make sure he is ready and able to fit in with the particular system by which it is run. It is no service to the teacher or the school if there is a mismatch. Recruits to the profession whose attitudes and skills equip them to play a significant and positive role within a flexible structure will find little but misery in a tightly structured environment. The converse is equally true. It is not always easy for candidates to find out exactly what makes a particular institution tick, but they ought to make a great effort to do so. In return, schools need to be much more forthcoming than they sometimes are about their priorities and emphases, not to mention their problems. I admit to finding myself out in some dubious practices. I used not to arrange interviews in the lunch period because that was the time when the children might be seen at their worst. Who was I fooling? Whoever was appointed would witness the situation within a few hours of taking up his post. What was more, he might even be on duty trying to deal with it. Better that he should know the truth *before* committing himself. The inner compulsion to present the school's most acceptable face is understandable but should be overcome. Professionalism demands that we tell the unvarnished truth. Similarly, candidates for posts must be ready to say how they feel about a school's style. I usually say something like this to those who come for interview at Eltham Green:

I want you to know this is a tightly organized school in which we believe in law and order. We take a very firm line with troublemakers and punish them severely. We test the children when they arrive and there's a good deal of setting. You won't find much mixed ability teaching around here. The headmaster is a pretty abrasive type and not easy to work with. Teachers who don't pull their weight are likely to be told the truth about themselves in the middle of the staffroom at morning break with everyone listening. We believe teachers and pupils need a clear structure within which to operate. If you are looking for the permissive society, you won't find it here. There are some very good schools which use a flexible approach. I will tell you where to find them if you like. This most definitely isn't one of them. Now, have I said enough to put you off? If so, goodbye and no hard feelings.

I offer this little sermon to all candidates for all posts, at whatever level. I adopted this approach in the early seventies when the profession seemed to be polarizing between two extreme styles of approach. Despite the shortage of teachers in those days, one had to be sure that the wrong people were not appointed. It is always better to have no teacher at all than one who is going to bring dissent into a school. If there is a divided staffroom, children soon catch the scent of it. Once a school loses its sense of direction, every possible disaster follows. The real tragedy of William Tyndale School was not that the staff all went the wrong way, but that they divided and went into two different directions. Had they been united in purpose and resolve, it just might have been a different story. Having said that, one has to acknowledge that young teachers coming out of colleges and institutes of education in the eighties will be faced with an immensely difficult situation. Many will be hard put to it to find any jobs at all; there will certainly not be much opportunity to exercise a choice. Despite that, one is still bound to urge caution upon them. If someone gets into the wrong style of school at the start, it can be the end of them.

My views on this subject derive from what can only be described as bitter experience. When I arrived at Eltham Green School in 1970, it was to a profoundly divided staff. There was no common philosophy except perhaps that of survival. There was a chasm between the traditionalists and the progressives which was quite unbridgable. The deputy head refused to acknowledge that the school had any problems at all, while the senior master catalogued them with unremitting perceptiveness. The local inspector kept telling me about the need to reconcile the different factions: a policy that would have been unwise even if it had not been manifestly impossible. Members of the inspectorate generally want peace at any price, but it is something that cannot be had. The cost of public peace between teachers who disagree about fundamentals is a sort of educational underground warfare. While that may appear to inspectors who are at some distance from the situation to be an improvement, it does not deceive children, who always know just what is going on in their school (and will even tell you what the notices in the staffroom say if you ask them).

It is not reasonable to expect a mature professional whose experience has led him to believe in (say) firm discipline, close obedience to school uniform regulations and the separation of children into ability groups, to work happily in harness with another mature professional who is committed to the complete opposite. There is, of course, no right or wrong about this. Each is thoroughly entitled to a particular view, and doubtless operates most effectively within its boundaries. And therein lies the problem. Reconciliation requires either that one position be abandoned completely or that each person surrender some territory. The latter would seem the more reasonable, but where does it lead? Usually a teacher's philosophy is all of a piece, with attitudes on discipline lining up with attitudes on teaching methods. Trying to reconcile the two approaches is like trying to fit the pieces of two different jigsaws together. In the end, tempers are lost and the whole thing ends up being thrown across the room. There is only one way of solving the problem of a divided staff: one of the two factions must be encouraged to go. The thirty or so teachers at Eltham Green who resigned at the end of my first term did so for the most part without acrimony. All but a few were good at their job and had very supportive testimonials and references from me. They found their right niche elsewhere in the education system, which was as much to their benefit as was their departure to Eltham Green's.

Those who saw my arrival as signalling a return to traditional standards – a sort of day of the reactionaries – misunderstood what was happening. There were many ways in which traditional approaches already had a firm hold on the school. A great fuss was made about school uniform, right down to the colour of the girls' knickers. An elaborate system of school and house prefects and sub-prefects existed. The need for bright children to have extensive GCE opportunities dominated the upper school timetable. People were caned for not doing their homework. There were declamations in classical languages at speech day – an occasion which only the smartest and best-behaved children were allowed to attend, the less desirable elements being put down in the workshops for the afternoon. None of this struck me as particularly progressive, and it was not clear at first what the educational *avant garde* feared from my coming. In most areas of the school's life, it would have been difficult to make things more traditional than they already were.

The real problem quickly became clear. There was no consistency of style throughout the school, each department being allowed to go its own way in deciding which attitudes to engender. Some teachers positively encouraged senior pupils to challenge and ignore school policies. No one who knows the condition of our education system will be surprised to hear that the English Department played a major role in this.

My arrival forced people to make up their minds about what they wanted, and to accept that a school cannot succeed if it tries to have things both ways. No school policy is any good unless it is implemented by everybody. This does not mean that everyone has to agree with it. Professionalism quite often means going along with things of which one disapproves, or departing to some other place where what one wishes to do is in tune with the institution concerned. When I explained this to one rather spiky liberal, she told me the third alternative was for her to stay and try to put a stop to what I was doing. She was fundamentally opposed to the authority of people like head teachers. Like many of that view, she exerted iron control over her classes and was far more totalitarian than any head under whom I have ever worked. She found it impossible to accept criticism and resented it strongly when spoken to about arriving late. She wanted, in fact, to be a law unto herself, and she represented a certain type of teacher who exerts a disturbing influence. In a large comprehensive, there are bound to be areas of difference between staff. It is the role of the leadership to decide which way to go. Those who cannot accept such an authority structure are ships of the destroyer class. The sooner they pass through one's stretch of ocean, the better.

Some of those who wished to challenge the school's apparent change of direction were confused about what was happening: they could not see how the pieces of the new jigsaw fitted together. One diminutive but very sound young man in the English Department kept telling his colleagues to wait before passing judgement. The worries of the not-sure-what-to-think group were set out in a letter written after he had visited the school by an ex-pupil from the Blackheath intelligentsia who had a Cambridge doctorate under his belt. Here are some extracts from his three pages of analysis:

Let me apologize in advance for the vehemence of my opinions – please put this down to my emotional vested interest in the school as a former pupil, not forgetting a rapidly developing professional interest as a potential probation officer . . . .

First of all I should admit my admiration for many of the structural changes you have made: de-streaming, year divisions instead of houses, social education. I feel somewhat disarmed as a critic in the face of what you have achieved . . . .

I *cannot* help thinking that Rony Robinson would have been wiser to adopt a wait-and-see position. After all, his novel is an attack on unfeeling comprehensive dinosaurs saturated in an appropriate mythology of academicism. The new Eltham Green, in spite of the beating policy, has a far more realistic view of its pupils needs. In my time there was never any question that caning might be dropped, so I cannot sympathize very much with the sudden fit of anti-caning hysteria which seems to have coincided with your arrival . . . .

As far as my own views are concerned, I regard hitting people as an admission of failure and inadequacy on the part of the teacher. Of course, our society is a narrowly punitive one; it would be surprising if teachers did not share the general outlook with its mistrust of human potential. An evangelical atheist like myself is inclined to trace the cultural influence back to the unfortunate Christian doctrine of original sin. There is justice in the fact that the beaters are a guilt-ridden lot of mediocrities. Those who wield the cane need to do so not because of the villainy of the offender but due to their own personality difficulties. The trouble is that school children are quick and cruel in the way that they find out and intimidate the weaker teachers. In this situation the need to punish soon arises. Teachers of this sort who actually fear children should be encouraged to leave the profession. Discipline does not mean physical punishment but firmness in following up offenders, consistency in attitude and treatment, combined with a simple willingness to talk openly and honestly to the various sub-cultures of rebellion. The latter (exemplified to a great extent in your own approach) should exclude the need for the former.

My first reaction was to publish the letter as an answer to all those who claimed that comprehensive schools were not teaching people to use the English language properly. Parts of it would have done justice to the most erudite of sociologists: those people whom Alistair Cooke says have translated 'boy meets girl' into 'intrapersonal familial relations'.

But despite his command of language, the writer seemed as hysterical about corporal punishment as those he criticized for being so. He was unable to perceive that, unless one happened to share his objection to it in principle, it was thoroughly in tune with his own definition of discipline as having to do with firmness and consistency. What he and many others could not understand, was how a man who was ready to communicate with and provide for the most rebellious elements in a way that they had never known before could, at the same time, visit a reign of terror upon them. There is in fact a paradox at the heart of the discipline question. It is this: there can only be real freedom where control has been established. Conversely, where freedom is given first priority, chaos will reign. Whether or not a teacher has discipline has nothing to do with whether or not his pupils are climbing the walls. The test comes when he tells them to come down. It is possible to give children the right to do anything – including climb the walls – if you are in control. But if you are not, only repression will avert chaos, and that not for long.

What the writer of that letter was worried about, as were those not-sure-what-to-think teachers at Eltham Green, was that I did not match any of their categorizations. The new messiah of the disadvantaged child should surely have been a kinder sort of chap. A senior member of staff (who meant no offence) said to me as we stood before a picture of my predecessor, 'Now *he* was a *gentle* man.' Someone placed this note in the box outside my study: 'Underneath that tough exterior lies a heart of stone.'

One of my favourite passages on the subject of being cruel in order to establish a basis for being kind comes from an address given to the Headmasters' Conference in 1963 by the late Donald Hughes of Rydal School. He reminded his hearers of the Gadarene swine into whom Jesus sent the evil spirits which had possessed the man Legion, after which the herd rushed down the hillside and were drowned in the sea:

> The Gardarene heresy regards the educational process as allowing your charges to run violently down a steep place and providing first aid at the bottom. The difficulty is that when the young run violently down steep places they drag others with them. Samson would make a good representative type of adolescent. He was very strong and very impetuous and his hair was never quite the right length. And he involved other people in his self-destruction and no one could pick up the pieces. Those who entrust children to our care have a right to expect that we shall not leave them to be the victims of one another's experiments in ethics. 'The burnt child dreads the fire' is a very useful cliché but it would be a very poor school motto. Please God we shall keep some of them out

of the fire altogether, even if we have to exercise a little authority to do so.

A change in the leadership of a school inevitably means the coming of a new authority style. The trauma which came upon the staffroom at Eltham Green in 1970 had its origins in that; but it was exacerbated by the divisions that already existed between teacher and teacher. The year 1970 was make-up-your-mind time. As those who rejected the new way of doing things took their departure, they were replaced by people who matched the new ethos that was being created. Thus does a school change from being one sort of place to being another: by movement of staff. It is a fact that one does well to bear in mind as the eighties unwind and many parents and politicians look for a different emphasis in the education system from the past.

The *cognoscenti* of our existing system identify the probationer teacher as the key to the future. Without question, one of the most significant developments in recent years has been a new concentration of attention and resources upon the teacher who is in his first appointment. No longer is the newcomer thrust in at the deep end and ignored until he screams for a lifebelt. The day of the probationer has arrived. However, the sort of provision some people think is required should be the subject of second thoughts. The induction schemes which have sprung up in London and elsewhere, by which young teachers are taken out of school to attend meetings and conferences every other week during their first year, satisfy the consciences of local authorities and inspectors without achieving very much. Indeed, the problems they present make one hesitate to appoint people straight from college. The time for teachers to be released from their commitments to discuss what teaching is all about is after they have had some considerable experience of it. It is astonishing that, after three or four years of lectures and seminars at college, it should be thought essential for people to be released within a few weeks of taking up their first appointments in order to spend more time talking about what they are supposed to be doing. The most important statement ever made about education came from the pen of Jean Piaget who wrote, 'I do, therefore I know'. He was thinking about how children learn, but it applies no less to teachers.

One does not question the need for young teachers to have every possible support and guidance during their first year, but the place for that is in school. Ask any member of the profession and he will tell you the same story: the only genuinely valuable part of his training was the teaching practice. The study of educational psychology may be of some significance after a year or two's experience in the classroom; before that, it is largely meaningless. The bulk of teacher training should come after someone has spent at least one full academic session teaching. Anyone who claims it would be unthinkable to place young recruits in the hands of schools on a full-time basis without a complete course of training beforehand shows an unwarranted lack of confidence in school heads of departments, most of whom are the best teacher-trainers to be found anywhere in our education system. They certainly have a much better appreciation of what is required in the classroom than those lecturing in colleges, many of whom are refugees from the chalkface. Those who have come back on to the school staffing market with the closure of college departments have confirmed one's worst fears. At interview, they show little or no awareness of classroom reality as it is today; if appointed, they present far greater problems than the average young probationer. A redundant senior lecturer quickly revealed that she had no idea how to control a class of perfectly ordinary children. The author of that letter from Blackheath would have spotted her at once as a creator of naughty boys and girls. In the early weeks, pupils appeared outside my door who had never been in any kind of trouble before and who were clearly puzzled about how they had managed to join the ranks of our regular troublemakers. 'Sir, I'm not sure what I did,' said one of our most exemplary young gentlemen, 'but it must have been something, or I wouldn't have been sent down here.' He was quite prepared to be punished for a misdemeanour he could not identify. As he puckered his brow at me, I couldn't help thinking he would have been at home in the ranks of the Light Brigade at Balaclava. I asked the teacher why she did not put into practice the advice she must have given her students about class control. 'Because,' she replied, 'it doesn't *work*.' She has since discovered otherwise, and become quite a good teacher, but it has been a steep haul. There is an unarguable case for regularly seconding college staff to teach in schools for a term or two so that they can remind themselves of what it is all about. There would be no shortage of experienced teachers prepared to exchange with them for a while and look at schools from the outside: an experience that would be invaluable, since it is possible to be too close to a situation for too long and thereby lose track of what is important.

The duties that a school owes to its probationers are three: to inform, to advise and to support. Of primary importance is the need to provide adequate information about how the institution is run. Some large comprehensives produce a staff brochure setting out the organization of the school and the procedures which apply. It takes a great weight off the mind of a young teacher to know exactly what to do in any situation and precisely what is allowed and what is not within the established style and ethos. This is especially true in the area of class control. Ask anyone about to begin his career in the classroom what is his greatest fear, and he will give you the answer in one word: discipline. On stepping in front of a class for the first time, we have all had the same worry: what to do if we cannot control them. That fear is immensely reduced if the person concerned knows in advance precisely what to do when there are problems, as there surely will be. Any school that leaves newcomers to find out as they go along what is and what is not acceptable invites trouble. That is not altogether rare, but there is a more common weakness. Some head teachers take the view that each member of staff must pick his own way through the disciplinary minefield, deciding for himself which route to take and being spoken to only when he adopts a procedure which is unacceptable. This democratic approach simply aggravates the fledgling's sense of insecurity at a time when he most needs a clear structure within which to operate.

At Eltham Green School, a ten-part staff brochure has evolved over the past decade. It sets out the academic and pastoral structures of the school, gives details of everyone's responsibilities, and explains disciplinary procedures. Ten practical hints are offered to young teachers in the matter of classroom discipline. They were drawn up in 1974 by senior members of staff with literally hundreds of years of experience between them.

1   Start right. Train your classes to line up outside classrooms and enter them in an orderly way.

2   Go properly equipped. Make sure you have with you everything you need for the lesson you have prepared. Do not send children on errands to fetch things: if you are disorganized your class will catch the same spirit.

3   Be equipped for the worst. It's a good idea always to have with you a box of pencils and a packet of paper for children who have come without their equipment, otherwise you may spend the first half of a lesson organizing loans between pupils. But leave five minutes at the end to get your property back.

4   Keep a register of each class and mark it before the lesson begins so that you know exactly who is there, and so that the children know that you know.

5   Reduce behaviour problems to individuals. Most unruly classes are like that because of one or two individuals. Mass punishments are usually ineffective. Thirty children do not mind being kept in together: there is a *camaraderie* of affliction in that situation. Hence, class detentions are NOT permitted at Eltham Green. The important thing is to isolate individuals. Here are some ways of doing that:

   (a) Separate your problem pupil within the classroom: put him at the front on his own and give him a special task to get on with while you teach the rest.

   (b) Put your problem pupil outside in the corridor. But first, make sure there is no one outside the door of another classroom in the same corridor: two villains in the corridor together spells trouble.

NB This should be regarded as a serious step, because a pupil outside your classroom is likely to be picked up by me or a senior member of staff and summarily punished.

(c) Ask a senior colleague next door or nearby to take your problem pupil into his or her class.

6   Only threaten once, then carry out your threat to the letter. For example, if you have said you will put a boy outside if he fools about again, do it the moment he repeats his offence. Never threaten what you cannot or do not intend to carry out. Never make repeated threats. Some experienced teachers would say never threaten at all, just go ahead and punish the first time a pupil offends. There is nothing wrong with that advice.

7   Set extra work. This is an effective sanction in the case of relatively able and well-behaved pupils whose behaviour has lapsed. It's no good for pupils of little ability or those who never get their work in on time anyway. You will end up by making work for yourself if you set additional assignments for boys and girls who will have to be chased for weeks afterwards to deliver the goods.

NB If you do set extra work, it must be in your own subject: it is unprofessional to use someone else's subject as a punishment. The setting of lines is NOT permitted.

8   Call in senior staff if you have persistent problems. We have *all* had discipline problems in our careers and there is nothing to be ashamed about if you have them. It's better to ask for help too soon than too late. Take particular note of the following:

(a) Your head of department is responsible for discipline within your department, so make sure he or she knows your problems.

(b) Also make sure a pupil's head of year is informed if there is serious and/or persistent trouble. Other departments may be complaining about the same pupil you are struggling with, in which case a red card will be issued.

These two points are very important. If you isolate yourself with your problems they will overwhelm you. Heads of departments and heads of years expect to be told what is going on: they are answerable if you have a disaster. Put notes in their pigeon-holes if you aren't going to see them soon after any disciplinary event.

9 In an emergency, stop everything. What troubles most young teachers is the question of what to do when a pupil (or sometimes a whole class) gets out of hand. If that happens, do one of these things:

(a) Ask your colleague next door to watch your class while you bring the offending pupil to the office wing to be dealt with. If the pupil can be relied on to report to the office wing without escort, send him down on his own. But if you do this, check afterwards that he got there.

(b) If a whole class becomes unmanageable, go and fetch the nearest senior member of staff (your head of department is first choice if nearby).

NB Before getting to situation (b), you might try stopping your carefully prepared lesson and making the whole class get their heads down to some writing (another reason for always having spare paper and pencils with you: see item 3 above).

10 Good discipline is not a matter of tricks. It is a matter of proper professional attention to the job in hand and an unremitting effort to master the art and science of teaching. Good discipline arises from self-discipline and it begins with the teacher: we must be disciplined ourselves if we are to get the behaviour we want from children. That means being on time, being prepared for whatever may happen, and insisting on good standards. Here is how to get good discipline: be punctual, be prepared, and be persistent.

Backing up information and advice must come support. The young teacher needs to know there is a ready ear and a willing presence to hear and act upon his problems (and also to acknowledge his triumphs). I make no apology for being an interfering headmaster, or for expecting my senior colleagues to be of the same mind. During the dark days of the early seventies, I was often accused of undermining the authority of teachers by going into their classrooms when there was chaos to sort things out (this did not stop short of my throwing desks and chairs across the room to demonstrate the seriousness of my intentions). A teacher's authority is much more likely to be permanently damaged by his inability to control his class than by any act of intervention. Of course, it depends how it is done. The important thing is to present a united front to boys and girls; to make it clear that the fault is all theirs (even if it is not and you are going to have to make that clear to the teacher in private afterwards). I recollect one occasion when I went into a noisy class and told them that Mr So-and-So was not going to be allowed to waste his time on them if they could not behave. He was, I explained, a highly qualified Bachelor of Arts from one of Europe's most distinguished universities, and they were lucky to have him. Any more trouble, and I would give him to some other class. Said one child as they came out of the room shortly afterwards, 'I didn't know he was as clever as all *that*.' Support means going to the same classroom week after week if there are problems; it sometimes means reorganizing classes to separate troublemakers from one another; it involves looking at the teaching material being used and many other things as well.

All of this is firstly the responsibility of heads of departments, but the head teacher must be involved as well. A large comprehensive calls for delegation of many responsibilities, but a head is on a dangerous road if he allows his attention to stray far from the daily classroom situation which is the heart and soul of his organization. It is all too easy to forget what are the concerns of the ordinary teacher. They are not to do with the grand sweep of educational philosophy, but with whether or not everyone has his exercise book and something to write with, because without these the most carefully prepared lesson can be brought to nought.

In a piece of research carried out by the National Association of Youth Clubs towards the end of the sixties and published under the title *The Unattached*, some girls were asked to express an opinion of their school teachers:

Although a feeling of resentment towards authority as such was apparent, the real focus of dislike was the teachers' poshness which the girls felt was often assumed in order to demonstrate that a social gap existed between teacher and pupil; they felt especially strongly against young members of staff on the grounds that not only did younger teachers not understand girls, but they did not want to understand them. It was easier to accept that someone of forty or fifty could not understand what it was like to be a teenager in the 1960s than it was to accept that someone in their twenties would not try to understand them. While some girls thought that only middle-aged people could effectively keep order among a mixed group of teenagers, they felt that only younger adults could understand them, if they cared to make the effort.

What is interesting about that passage is not only the picture it draws of teachers, but also what it says about teenage girls who attend youth clubs. They are often the ones who have got least out of school and have been most anxious to put it behind them. The idea that teachers are a posh lot is common enough among such young people.

The more general image of teachers has little to do with poshness, especially now that the seventies have been and gone. In a decade which brought schools closer than ever before to the communities in which they have their being, a new picture of the classroom practitioner has slowly emerged. It is not yet clearly drawn, but some of the features are sharp enough to be distinguished without difficulty. The young secondary schoolmasters and schoolmistresses of the eighties will have three characteristics among others. Firstly, they will have been educated in a comprehensive school and will therefore know much more about the real world in which all kinds of children live than many of their predecessors. Secondly, they will have thought very carefully about entering the profession before doing so. In the sixties and early seventies sixth-formers frequently went to train as teachers because they were not up to university entrance. It was a generally recognized way of staying in the education system if you had up to that point been happy in it and achieved some success. But it caused many young people to become teachers by default, which is not the best way. Such a situation will not continue, given the shortage of teaching posts available. The third characteristic of the teacher of the eighties will be an inclination to close ranks with colleagues. The tripartite system produced a tripartite profession. Those subtle distinctions (and sometimes not-so-subtle ones), which have traditionally separated one teacher from another, are gradually disappearing as comprehensivization turns schools into something like the real world. In due course, even those who teach engineering subjects will find a proper value placed on their contribution to education.

But whatever changes overtake the image of a teacher, the task will remain a highly individual one. When it comes to the daily classroom drama, the performance is delivered by you alone with thirty of them and the door shut. We educators are all virtuosos at heart. In the summer of 1973, André Previn gave a television lecture on the subject 'Who Needs a Conductor?' Having explored the various influences which seemed to suggest that having someone at the front telling everyone what to do was an obsolete concept, he ended with some words that will strike a chord in the heart of all teachers:

> The days of the maestro are over. Nevertheless, under that new, self-effacing, I-am-one-of-the-boys, merely-a-tool-of-the-gods exterior, lies a heart of pure vanity.

Without becoming unnecessarily vain, every classroom practitioner needs a certain belief in his own unique contribution to the education process. For, in the final analysis, it is not so much what he offers his class as the response it creates that matters most. The most carefully constructed lesson, delivered with the greatest professional aplomb, will achieve little if it leaves children in that state of semi-conscious bliss in which, given the choice, they would choose to spend their days. It was said of Cicero that, when he had finished speaking, the people would declare, 'How well he spoke.' But after hearing

Demosthenes they would say, 'Let us march.' It is the demosthenic response the teacher must be after. Those anxious examinations of function which are urged upon us from some quarters are unnecessary. One's principal activity is a straightforward scientific one: to generate a controlled reaction. Some fear reaction means loss of control; others that control will inhibit reaction. The skill that has to be learned is concerned with having both.

George S. Kaufman pointed out that, if matches had been invented *after* cigarette lighters, they would have been the sensation of the century. Which way round the truth comes to us is of no small importance. A broad philosophy, articulated in erudite terms, is doubtless a most important possession for a teacher; but his initial thinking needs to be concentrated on how to earn a response from children within a structure where it can be directed to useful ends. That primary principle must be discovered first if the science of teaching, which is also an art, is to prosper.

Six

Pupils

Mr Quelch pointed to the Latin dictionary on the table: 'Bunter! You placed this book on my door, to fall when I entered my study!' Billy Bunter jumped. This was quite unexpected. He would not have been surprised to hear something about biscuits missing in the common room or bananas from a fifth-form study. But this did surprise him. He goggled at Quelch.

Thus began one more story of disaster for the Owl of the Remove at Greyfriars School. Not for the first time, the fat boy created by Frank Richards had failed to deceive his astute and perceptive form master. The tale continued:

Five fellows were waiting for him when he emerged tottering into the quad. But if Harry Wharton and Co had hostile intentions, they forgot them at the sight of the suffering Owl. In fact his aspect might have melted a heart of stone.

'Hallo, hallo, hallo!' exclaimed Bob Cherry. 'What – ?'

'Ow! Ow! Oooch! I – I say, you fellows, Quelch knew it was me – wow! I say, I've had – wooh! – six! Wow! Ow! Oooh! Oh, crikey! Did he lay it on! Wow!'

'Ha, ha, ha!'

'Blessed if I can see anything to cackle at! I tell you I've had six – wow!'

'Serve you jolly well right!' said Johnny Bull.

'The rightfulness is terrific, my esteemed fat Bunter.'

'Ow! Beast! Wow!'

The fact that, in the opinion of the Famous Five, it served him right, did not seem to comfort Billy Bunter in the very least. It was a sad, suffering, sorrowful Owl.

Those whose Christmas reading as children was *Greyfriars Annual* did not actually believe such places and such people existed.. Bunter, Biggles and Batman have each given young people many enjoyable hours precisely because they operate outside the limitations of normal human existence. A minute or two after making all that fuss, Billy would be tucking into an enormous pie, stuffing himself with sausages, or devouring huge quantities of ice cream, with no hard feelings against anyone. None of his escapades was really disruptive – that would have been quite improper – and there were no genuinely unpleasant relationships at the old school. To coin a phrase that would have appealed to no less a person than Harry Wharton himself, everyone got on famously. But those who avidly devoured the adventures of Harry and his cohorts knew the real world was not like that.

A rather different sort of Billy is Barry Hines' creation in *A Kestrel for a Knave*. He waits outside the headmaster's study with MacDowell to be punished for misbehaving in assembly. Three smokers are there too. MacDowell complains to Billy Casper about life's injustice.

> 'It wasn't me that coughed tha knows. I'm going to tell him so an' all.'
> 'It makes no difference whether tha tells him or not, he don't listen.'
> 'I'm bringing my father up if he giz me t'stick, anyroad.'
> 'What tha allus bringin' thi father up for? He never does owt when he comes. They say t'last time he came up, Gryce gave him t'stick an' all.'
> The three smokers fell away and leaned back on the half-tiled wall to observe.
> 'At least I've got a father to bring up, that's more than that can say, Casper.'
> 'Shut thi gob, MacDowall!'

This is a very different world from that of Harry Wharton and Co. Within a few pages of the beginning of the story, Billy Casper falls in the dog shit climbing a fence; makes a V sign and farting noise at his mother; calls his brother a drunken bastard. This is the stuff of which examination set books are made.

Without question, the life of Billy Casper reflects actuality in a way that Billy Bunter was never intended to. And yet, his story is a long way from being representative of how the average child lives. The unloved and underachieving youngster who presents such an interesting subject for the modern novelist and social commentator does not typify general reality. It is as misleading to persuade ordinary children to see life in Billy Casper's terms as it is to invite them to believe in Greyfriars. It is claimed that Barry Hines' novel is a real slap in the face for those who believe that orange juice and comprehensive schools have taken the meanness out of life. But for most children, life is not mean but interesting and exciting. They know themselves to be cared for at home, and they find school an enjoyable experience.

It was once alleged that a certain Secretary of State for Education and Science made the comprehensive sound like a cross between a soup kitchen and the Hospital for Tropical Diseases. But it is not always those who have no experience of such schools who misrepresent them. Teachers seem sometimes to get a perverse satisfaction from relating the worst they have to endure, rather than what is the norm. The staffroom in the average state secondary is always full of the most astonishing tales of disaster and near-disaster. Their impact is heightened because the profession has a high proportion of excellent raconteurs whose gift for making the ordinary into something dramatic is a wonder to behold. Nor do they hesitate to relate their stories to friends and neighbours, a certain glory being available to those seen as daily survivors of the comprehensive holocaust. Perhaps it is not all that surprising that a girl was called comprehensive trash by her fellow university students from public schools.

Most children in a comprehensive school are in no way extraordinary or remarkable. The trouble is, public attention is rarely attracted by the ordinary: it is drama that draws the crowd and sells the newspapers. Widespread news coverage was given to the fact that one of Inner London's most prestigious comprehensives, Pimlico School, employed security guards. The fact that Sir Ashley Bramall, Leader of the Inner London Education Authority, was closely associated with the school gave bite to the story. A reporter who was interested in widening its implications rang to ask me if we had any security guards at Eltham Green. 'Yes,' I replied, 'one – me.' There was a pause as the caller reflected on my reply. He said that I was not taking him seriously. I suggested that, if he wanted to do a really serious piece of reporting on the condition of the school, he was welcome to come down with a photographer and see for himself a large number of children behaving themselves and enjoying their lessons. His reply deserves to be recorded: 'If everything's alright, we're not interested.'

Had that reporter accepted my invitation, he would have been able to see inside a comprehensive school with one considerable advantage over many others: a precisely balanced intake of pupils drawn in the right proportions from different parts of the ability spectrum. The biggest single handicap from which a comprehensive school can suffer is not having a genuinely comprehensive intake. It was one of the many difficulties facing Eltham Green School in 1970. How the situation changed in ten autumns is an important part of the story of its journey from darkness into light.

To understand what happened requires some knowledge of the system used in Inner London in the seventies for transferring children from primary schools to comprehensive schools. Early in a pupil's final year of primary education, an assessment was made by his school which specified his ability in verbal reasoning (VR), English and mathematics. In each he was placed, as has been mentioned before, either in the upper twenty-five per cent (Group 1), the middle fifty per cent (Group 2) or the lower twenty-five per cent (Group 3).

In November of his final year, he and his contemporaries took an official VR test. This was done anonymously, the scores simply being tabulated and sent to those qualified to interpret the significance of such things at County Hall. A ten per cent sample went to the National Foundation of Education Research for the creation of a conversion table, to take account of age differences.

In January, similar tests were taken in English and mathematics and the tabulated results sent to County Hall.

Having been provided with all this data, the Inner London Education Authority, determined for each primary school the number of children who should rightly be placed in each group in the three designated areas of ability, taking account of how boys and girls compared with those elsewhere. This information was communicated on or about St Valentine's Day, but did not invariably generate love and goodwill. Primary heads who found they had allocated too few or too many children to a particular group in their original assessments were expected to reconsider the position, but that was not mandatory.

On the basis of the VR information provided, a divisional formula for each part of Inner London was devised each year. This showed the spread of ability between the three groups that should have been reflected in any form of thirty children entering a comprehensive school in the locality. The formula was set out as a 1 : 2 : 3 ratio, showing the number of children who ought to fall into each ability group. For example, the divisional formula for Eltham Green in 1979 was 9 : 15½ : 5½. meaning that each form of thirty pupils should have contained nine children with VR 1, fifteen or sixteen with VR 2 and five or six with VR 3. The basic divisional formula was translated into an overall figure for a school's intake. The 1979 position at Eltham Green was therefore as follows:

| Basic Divisional Formula | 9 | : | 15½ | : | 5½ | = | 30 |
| Formula for Total Intake | 99 | : | 171 | : | 60 | = | 330 |

Given this system, or any other which attempts to provide comprehensive schools with properly balanced intakes without direction of pupils, there will be one essential precondition for a particular establishment to recruit the right spread of ability: it must be oversubscribed. The figures for Eltham Green which are set out in Table 5 tell their own story. In the years 1976 to 1980 recruitment was so close to the divisional formula that people frequently expressed astonishment at the near-infallibility of the

Table 5: Recruitment at Eleven

Year	Proposed Intake	Total Applicants	Oversubscription by VR Groups 1 : 2 : 3							
1970	390	273	Undersubscribed							
1971	390	347	Undersubscribed							
1972	390	360	Undersubscribed							
1973	360	343	Undersubscribed							
1974	330	368	Applicants	54	:	211	:	103	=	368
			Divisional formula	64	:	187	:	79	=	330
			Accepted	54	:	191	:	88	=	333
1975	330	387	Applicants	66	:	215	:	106	=	387
			Divisional formula	65	:	183	:	82	=	330
			Accepted	60	:	179	:	91	=	330
1976	330	385	Applicants	74	:	203	:	108	=	385
			Divisional formula	73	:	179	:	78	=	330
			Accepted	74	:	175	:	81	=	330
1977	360	438	Applicants	130	:	209	:	99	=	438
			Divisional formula	102	:	180	:	78	=	360
			Accepted	102	:	177	:	81	=	360
1978	330	429	Applicants	126	:	219	:	84	=	429
			Divisional formula	86	:	174	:	70	=	330
			Accepted	87	:	172	:	71	=	330
1979	330	411	Applicants	132	:	219	:	60	=	411
			Divisional formula	99	:	171	:	60	=	330
			Accepted	103	:	167	:	60	=	330
1980	330	364	Applicants	105	:	185	:	75	=	365
			Divisional formula	89	:	172	:	69	=	330
			Accepted	89	:	172	:	69	=	330

NOTES

1 In 1970 the Inner London Education Authority resolved to reduce the intake of the school from 13 forms (390 pupils) to 11 forms (330 pupils) owing to recruitment difficulties, this decision to be implemented by 1974.

2 In 1974 the school became oversubscribed for the first time in its history, although there was still a shortfall of 10 in Group 1 applications.

3 In 1975 the school became oversubscribed in all ability groups.

4   In 1977 the intake was temporarily raised to 12 forms (360 pupils) because of pressure for places at the school.

5   The figures in the third column need to be seen in relation to the falling rolls situation. The sustained national decline in births from 1964 to 1977 had the following effect on numbers transferring from primary to secondary schools in the divisional catchment area from 1975 onwards:

1976: 72 fewer than previous year   1979: 160 fewer than previous year
1977: 143 fewer than previous year   1980: 106 fewer than previous year
1978: 54 fewer than previous year

Thus, in 1980 there were 535 fewer children on the move in the division than in 1975 (this within overall divisional figures which declined from about 3,700 to about 3,200).

system. The statistics certainly look impressive if one covers the top line of each series in the right-hand column and sees only the relationship between the bottom two lines. I recollect a conversation in the staffroom in 1978 when I had just published the divisional formula (86 : 174 : 70) and our actual intake for the coming September (87 : 172 : 71). 'It's very clever,' said a not-inexperienced teacher, 'how on earth did they get it so close?' The answer is, of course, they didn't. The people to be thanked for making a balanced intake possible were the parents of all the children who had been turned away.

There is a contradiction within any system that tries to combine choice with balance. The likelihood that balanced intakes will arise in some way from the unhindered exercise of parental options is so unrealistic as to be laughable. In effect, only a few schools in any area will receive children of different abilities in the right proportions on the basis of what parents choose. For example, of the nineteen comprehensives in Greenwich, fourteen were left with vacancies in one ability group or another in 1979. The very success of some schools in the matter of recruitment was made possible by the failure of others. That is a disturbing thought, since having a properly comprehensive collection of boys and girls is the starting point for providing properly comprehensive education.

Eltham Green did not become a comprehensive school until the middle of the seventies. As it moved from imbalance to balance, the attitude of pupils to one another and to their teachers changed. The arrival and influence of a considerable body of able children contributed to this. The proportion of those with a Grade 1 in one or more of the designated areas of ability rose from 24.5 per cent in 1974 to 30 per cent in 1975, 37 per cent in 1976 and 40 per cent in 1977. At the same time, the school's reputation for emphasizing what some saw as the old-fashioned standards of good behaviour and hard work was attracting children from homes and, no less significantly, from primary schools were such values had an important place. In the battles parents fought to get their children into the school – sometimes from places which were declared to be outside its catchment area and from primary schools that had been warned off – this was made clear time and time again.

The question of where the pupils to feed a comprehensive school should come from is one which has exercised the minds of politicians and administrators both sides of the Atlantic. Matching the local divisional formula will not make a school comprehensive if the community in which it stands produces a ratio of 2 : 12 : 16, as might well be the case in some parts of our inner cities. Transporting children daily from one area to another seems unlikely to be the English solution, although it does in a sense apply already wherever parents are permitted to choose a school other than their nearest one. Given the decay of inner city public transport, it is likely that in the eighties local authorities will have to review their eleven-plus transfer systems on grounds other than educational ones. The neighbourhood comprehensive does have one great advantage over all others: its pupils can actually reach it, even in the winter. Some of them may not be too enthusiastic about that, which is another reason for considering it. The problem of truancy is greatly exacerbated where a school draws from an area any significant distance from its immediate locality. It would not be unrealistic to attribute fifty per cent of the persistent absenteeism in any large inner city comprehensive to the excuse offered by the bus service. Most of those carrying senior pastoral responsibility in schools, who therefore have close daily acquaintance with late lines and similar phenomena, will confirm that opinion.

There are two further important questions to do with the way schools find their pupils which deserve attention. Firstly, one needs to ask to what extent alternatives to the large comprehensive should be preserved. Secondly, there is the matter of providing for those with special needs.

When I am asked whether I think any more schools for two thousand pupils should be built, my answer is, 'Yes, provided only fifteen hundred people are put in them.' What is important is not the number of boys and girls but the relationship between them and the space available. When we have reached the stage – and falling rolls are bringing us all to it – where there are rooms to spare in our schools, plus the further bonus of ample space in corridors and on staircases, something significant will have happened. The trouble with people who plan schools is they do not have to work in them. Of course, one realizes that financial restraints dictate the need to ensure the design size of a school matches its intake, but, as my old grandmother used to say, a little bit of something left over comes in handy.

For lack of something left over, some children suffer. There are those who find a large school, teeming with life in every corner, rather a lot to take. Every year there are one or two children like that at Eltham Green, and I have no hesitation in arranging for them to swim into quieter waters nearby. There is in my opinion an unarguable case for preserving some small schools for those youngsters who find that big is not beautiful. But that is not to say that most ordinary children are not perfectly happy in a large establishment. Those who attack the largeness of some comprehensives show, by their questions, that they have never spent any time in one. There are two queries commonly raised by such people. The first goes something like this: 'Don't you think children suffer from being in such large classes?' It took me some time after moving into the comprehensive sector to discover that such questioners believed a big school must have larger classes than a small school. The other question often comes from over-anxious members of the intelligentsia: 'You can't possibly *know* all the children in your school, can you?' This is usually followed up by some comparison with the traditional grammar school of six hundred pupils in which the head knew everyone. But he did not. It is merely part of the traditional mythology of the tripartite system. The grammar school head perhaps knew every pupil's name, but the close daily awareness of home background and circumstances possessed by today's typical comprehensive school head of year was quite unknown to him. Boys and girls in a large comprehensive with a well-organized pastoral system are better known, more closely watched, and invariably better cared for than youngsters used to be in the grammar school where my teaching career began. They have to be: they have far more problems. Or have they? We used not to find out about pupils' difficulties at the other place: it wasn't part of our professional responsibility.

Accepting pastoral care as the full professional responsibility of schools is one of the greatest achievements of the comprehensive system. There must be thousands of children whose head of year or head of house or some such person provides them with a daily life-support system. The time and attention given to children, and to the families from which they come, through comprehensive school pastoral structures goes far beyond anything available in the old style schools.

Whether there are children who should be provided for outside the ordinary comprehensive structure became an issue of great importance in the seventies, the debate reaching its climax with the publication of the Warnock Report in the spring of 1978. It is interesting to trace the history of the thinking behind its title: *Special Educational Needs*. At the beginning of the decade, those most closely concerned with making plans for children who presented problems in school were talking and writing, as was customary, in terms not of their needs but of their difficulties. Thus, for example, the Inner London Education Authority produced a lengthy report in the summer of 1971 entitled *Children with Special Difficulties*. What might be called the new thinking received clear expression when Warnock called for Sections 5 and 8 of the 1944 Education Act to be amended 'to embody a broader concept of special education related to a child's individual needs as distinct from his disability'. In short, too much emphasis had been given in the past to establishing what was wrong with children and not enough to meeting their condition. Few who have attempted to obtain special provision for problematic pupils will argue with that proposition. The cumbersome machinery that exists to ascertain children for special school placement leaves their needs unattended for weeks, months and even years, while their particular difficulties are identified. Then, after all the necessary experts have been consulted, appropriate reports submitted and meetings held, there is as often as not no provision available. From start to finish, it took just over a year for one of my boys to be declared maladjusted, and a further two years to find him a suitable placement. Most head teachers would be able to tell a similar story. It is a matter of fact that special education as it has been understood in the past has failed to meet the needs of a great many children who might reasonably have expected some help from it.

The new picture drawn by the members of the Warnock Committee has two principal features. Firstly, it broadens the definition of special education so that it 'extends beyond the idea of education provided in special schools, special classes or units for children with particular types of disability, and embraces the notion of *any form of additional help, wherever it is provided,* from birth to maturity, to overcome educational difficulty'. The italics are mine. Given such a definition, it is not unreasonable to claim that a good teacher provides special education all the time. Certainly, a great deal of the curriculum in a comprehensive school falls into that category. The distinction between what is special education and what is not becomes almost impossible to draw.

In an attempt to draw the line and quantify what should be the extent of special provision, Warnock suggests that about one in five children will at some time in their school careers require special educational help of one kind or another. In an ordinary comprehensive school, it is about right to say that half a dozen children in any class of thirty need more support than the rest.

There will be one or two requiring a very significant remedial component in their programmes throughout their school careers; there will be another one or two whose behaviour problems land them up in the school sanctuary unit or in some kind of off-site support centre; there will be a further one or two who might well be destined to find their place in a special school because of the development of severe physical or emotional disorders. If anything, the Warnock estimate is over-optimistic. It is partly based on information collected in Inner London in 1971, which is unlikely to tell us how things stand now and, more important, how they are likely to develop in the eighties. I suspect most head teachers would say the proportion of problematic pupils in schools is rising rather than falling or remaining constant.

The second principal feature of the Warnock recommendations concerns the future relationship between ordinary schools and special schools. This should, it is suggested, be much closer than in the past, and ought to involve joint planning of curriculum and timetables so that children may move easily between the two. One particular recommendation illustrates the thinking very clearly:

> . . . when any new special schools are built in the future, consideration should be given to constructing them in close proximity to ordinary schools so as to facilitate the development of positive collaboration between the two types of school.

The idea of collaboration, with special school children spending some time in an ordinary school and *vice versa*, is long overdue. But it calls for a completely new approach to methods of placement. At present, it is both extremely difficult to get a child into a special school and, once he is there, equally difficult to get him out again. The lengthy and ponderous procedures, plus the fact that final judgement rests with people in the medical, psychological and psychiatric services who are far removed from the classroom situation, make head teachers reluctant to seek placements. As a result, there has been created during the seventies an alternative special school structure within the ordinary school system – a development which has been largely initiated and carried through by comprehensive schools faced with solving their own problems.

Shortly after we set up a sanctuary at Eltham Green, a group of American visitors happened to be in the school. When I mentioned the unit to them, they assumed it was for staff. It was, they thought, an excellent idea to have such a place for teachers who couldn't face it any more. 'But', said one of them, 'in New York you wouldn't have anybody left teaching in the classrooms.'

This story is a reminder that things are not always what they seem: a fact of life that especially applies to some of the ways schools try to deal with pupils who cause problems. Communicating exactly what you are up to in a way that can be generally understood is no easy matter. The man who runs the sanctuary unit at Eltham Green School rarely allows his pupils to depress him, difficult as some of them are: it is the staff who get him down. The tenacity with which they cling to the view that he is simply the keeper of a sin bin – a sort of educational garbage collector – tests his patience to the limit. Without doubt, a certain immunity to the uncomprehending attitude of one's professional colleagues is an essential qualification for working with problem pupils.

The reason why teachers take a limited view of sanctuary provision has to do with its two different functions, only one of which is readily understood. A school that has a unit into which disruptive pupils can be withdrawn for long or short periods appears to give precedence to ordinary, reasonably well-behaved children. Generally speaking, what makes it difficult to teach some classes is the presence of one or two individuals with an inclination to wreck things. Get them out of it and the education process can proceed relatively unhindered. Every teacher has known the experience of feeling his heart sink when a certain boy or girl arrives for a lesson. Rony Robinson catches the situation perfectly in his novel *The Ted Carp Tradition*:

Martin Closely came in and Mr Fitzjohn tried to smile.

'Good morning, Closely. How do you think they will do on Saturday? I've got them down for a draw. If they keep the ball moving'.

'Give over,' Closely muttered, spitting as he pushed past and went to his window seat. Football was the only sane string between them, so one of Mr Fitzjohn's professional duties this year had been a detailed study of the football pages, which he detested. Closely sometimes talked to him, especially when Manchester United had a good run. It was worth it even to get 'Give over'. It meant that he was probably alright for this lesson. Closely looked seventeen and was twelve. And mean.

The relief provided by the occasional withdrawal of the Closelys has been experienced by some of the best teachers. For those less good, it makes the difference between being able to go on and giving up. The existence of a sanctuary unit transforms the ordinary classroom situation and alters the tempo and effectiveness of normal day-to-day teaching. That much is easily understood. What is not is the role of whoever takes on the Closelys. The average teacher seems to find it hard to appreciate that anything beyond containment is possible for such pupils. The notion that they have special needs that should be met is not easily grasped: perhaps an understandable reaction when half the staff of a school has been driven to distraction by them. A dismissive attitude towards troublemakers penetrates all corners of special provision. Those who run the various alternative types of off-site unit that sprang up during the seventies – guidance centres, support centres, intermediate treatment centres and the like – find it not at all easy to place children back in school once their period of special tuition has ended. The tactics that some head teachers use to keep their miscreants at bay are audacious. During the two years of my responsibility for our local support centre immediately after its inception, there were a number of occasions when a school that was due to take back one of its pupils would say something like, 'Oh! Is *he* supposed to come back *here*? I hadn't realized that.' This was actually uttered with an emphatic note of surprise and a slight catch in the voice suggesting that tears were about to be shed. Yet the nineteen schools that used the centre all knew perfectly well that pupils went there for only six weeks, with a possible extension to twelve. Hope springs eternal in the human breast, and there is always the possibility that the nuisance you have got rid of will somehow or other disappear into the educational equivalent of outer space. There is hypocrisy in these words, for I am no less inclined than any other head teacher to offer silent prayers that some problems may never return. That being so, it is all the more understandable that the ordinary teacher takes the view he sometimes does of what a school sanctuary unit is for − simply to keep troublemakers off everyone else's back. It will perhaps always be the destiny of those working in them to have their efforts undervalued.

It is appropriate that the needs of the ordinary, average child should take first place in a school, and that they should be seen so to do. Is it possible to identify those needs in precise terms? What should the English education system be offering to the vast majority of pupils? In the matter of determining what young people need, Benjamin Franklin tells a cautionary tale. In the middle of the eighteenth century, the government of Virginia offered to give six places at their college in Williamsburg to young Red Indian braves so that they might be properly educated. The reply to this offer (as retold by Peter Medway in *The Receiving End*) was as follows:

> We know that you highly esteem the kind of learning taught in your colleges, and that the maintenance of our young men, while with you, would be very expensive to you. We are convinced, therefore, that you mean to do us good by your proposal and we thank you. But you, who are wise, must know that different nations have different conceptions of things; and you will not therefore take it amiss, if our ideas of this kind of education happen not to be the same as yours. We have had some experience of it; several of our young people were formerly brought up at the colleges of the northern provinces; they were

instructed in all your sciences; but, when they came back to us, they were bad runners, ignorant of every means of living in the woods, unable to bear either cold or hunger, knew neither how to build a cabin, take a deer, nor kill an enemy, spoke our language imperfectly, were therefore neither fit for hunters, warriors nor counsellors; they were totally good for nothing. We are, however, not the less obligated by your kind offer, though we decline accepting it, and to show our grateful sense of it, if the gentlemen in Virginia will send us a dozen of their sons, we will take care of their education, instruct them in all we know, and make men of them.

Not only do different nations have different conceptions of things; different political parties, local authorities and individual schools see education in different ways. That being so, what can be said that might have general application to the average child within our education system at the present time? While it is the role of the comprehensive school to provide for all types of children, that should not lead to neglect of the majority while attention is given to minority groups. If a comprehensive structure is only able to control the miscreant, stretch the high flyer and support the backward by neglecting the ordinary pupils who fall into none of those categories, going comprehensive has all been a ghastly mistake.

What is the ordinary pupil like, and what are his characteristics and his needs? He is generally someone who quite enjoys school and who would not consider playing truant. He likes some lessons better than others, his attitude depending on the quality of teaching, of which he is a very good judge. Without perhaps being fully aware of it, he is inclined to select his examination subjects on the basis of how well or badly he has been taught rather than because of any innate liking for one thing or another. This creates problems when, after being taught well in his third year in a particular subject, he moves up into an examination group that is less well taught and finds he has chosen wrongly. Heads of departments exacerbate this situation by giving their most promising third-year classes to their best teachers in the cause of examination recruitment. Any head of department who denies doing this is either dishonest or such a paragon of virtue as to put the rest of us to shame.

The average pupil, despite being well aware when he has a poor teacher, will rarely step beyond the bounds of messing about into the more dangerous territory of lesson-wrecking. He is in fact a most patient creature who will put up with a great deal unless provoked either by genuine miscreants around him in the classroom or truly abominable teaching. It is easier for a school to do something about the former than the latter. When ordinary children get into serious trouble in the classroom, the principal fault usually lies with the teacher.

If it is true, as some would claim, that the average child's standard of behaviour has declined in recent years, it is a judgement on those who stand at the blackboard rather than on those who sit in the desks. The ordinary youngster will, without being unduly enthusiastic about his lessons and his homework, do what is asked of him if he knows his teachers mean business. He will not, however, be long deceived by the pretences practised upon him by members of staff who are too idle or disorganized to check that work has been done. He becomes impatient if he has to wait a long time for exercises and essays to be marked, and loses any keenness he had to discover how well he performed. He is amused when he sees that a teacher cannot remember from one lesson to the next what material has been covered, then becomes irritated when this means going over the same work twice and sometimes three times. He notes with a cynicism beyond his years that some teachers talk a great deal about the need for children to be conscientious but fail by about the length of the Great Wall of China to live up to the demands they make on others. Conversely, he offers respect and affection to those who do him the honour of arriving on time, preparing lessons carefully, and marking work punctiliously. Here's a piece of advice for any young teacher who wants to be highly regarded by a class: get their homework back to them within a few days of their handing it in. This will earn you more applause than any amount of matey chat about how much you love teaching them.

It is alleged that a notice over a school fire alarm read, 'In event of fire, vandalize glass.' The popular image of the comprehensive school as a hotbed of vandalism does a grave injustice to ordinary boys and girls. They are not given to destruction of property, playground violence, abuse of adults, terrorizing the local neighbourhood, or any of the many other activities which have become part of comprehensive folklore. The vast majority of children indulge in none of these things. Indeed, so far as respect for property is concerned, they will observe very high standards if encouraged to do so. Children will match up to whatever we show we expect of them. If we allow ARSENAL to remain on the school wall, we are saying that writing on walls does not matter. Within twenty-four hours, the whole of the first division is likely to appear, with comments upon the relative worthiness of each team expressed in uninhibited terms. The rose beds at Eltham Green School are a source of great pride, not merely to the groundsman and teaching staff but to the vast majority of pupils too. But they did not reach their present condition without some difficulty. When standard roses were first planted on the main terrace where hundreds of children gather each day, I was warned they would not last a week. The first two or three weeks were indeed hard ones. By dint of constant vigilance, the few wreckers who laid hands on the young plants were caught and dealt with. They spent hours of their time hoeing the school flower beds to keep them immaculate. Their peers witnessed this, and on occasions gathered round to pass comments upon the manner in which they were carrying out their agricultural duties (an experience endured by every gardener). No one was left in any doubt that our rose beds were to be respected, and so they are.

Visitors to the school often comment on the cleanliness and good condition of the main building and the splendid lawns and flower beds surrounding it. 'You must', said someone from an institute of education, 'have very nice children here.' They are, in fact, perfectly ordinary children whose natural desire and inclination is, like that of all normal people, to live in pleasant surroundings. The school has done no more than provide a structure within which that ambition may be realized.

The investigation of what the average child is like makes his school needs plain: good teachers and an environment that earns his respect. His requirements in the two other major areas of his life, his home and eventually his place of work, are similar. For lack of the right people to care for him, or for want of a situation in which he feels able to respect what is around him, the normal child becomes abnormal and problematical. Paradoxically, the normal child's needs are not infrequently neglected while attention is given to those with profound problems. Thus do we create that which we seek to cure.

Seven

Care and Support

It is a traumatic experience for a parent to dispatch a vulnerable eleven-year-old into the giant maw of a massive comprehensive school. The annual assurance we offer is an essential part of the exercise: 'Don't worry: we will take good care of your child. Those tears you shed at the gate will be for yourself.' But parents have good reason for thinking their youngsters might be overwhelmed or overlooked. We in the schools do not serve our own best purposes by blandly pretending there is nothing for anyone to worry about. Big is not always beautiful, any more than small is always sensible. But there is no longer any serious cause for concern. The large comprehensive has discovered the secret of what is known in the trade as pastoral care. This is one of its greatest contributions to the development of the English education system.

Something which small schools, and especially selective ones, thought they did not have to worry about was the likelihood of neglecting the particular needs of the individual child. Everyone knew everyone else and no one was overlooked or misunderstood. The large school, with an intake ranging across the full social and ability spectrum, could not afford to make such assumptions. Unless positive steps were taken to incorporate a systematic framework for providing pastoral care within the organization, the individual would be swallowed by the monster. Partly because it was familiar, and partly for reasons of prestige, many of the early comprehensives adopted the house system as the basis of pastoral care. It bore an attractive association with grammar and public schools and seemed the obvious way of breaking down a large unit. When the Inner

111

London Education Authority published a report on the organization of its comprehensive schools in 1966, most of its large, purpose-built, best known and most prestigious institutions had house systems of one kind or another. But some, it was reported, had already abandoned this style of organization. One such was Walworth School, where Guy Rogers was conducting a most distinguished headship. During the seventies, there has been an increasing tendency for schools to move over to a horizontal structure in their pastoral arrangements.

At the time of my arrival in 1970, Eltham Green School operated an eight-house system. The names of the houses were, to say the least, unusual: Endeavour, Loyalty, Truthfulness, Honesty, Ambition, Modesty, Generosity, Sincerity.

Looking through a copy of the school magazine in preparation for taking up my appointment, I was amused by the opening sentence of one house report: 'Modesty has not shone very brightly this year.' One of the problems with house systems is that they are artificial creations superimposed upon a school's organization rather than arising naturally from its function as a teaching institution. The members of Honesty were no more honest than the rest, just as the members of Drake House at my first school felt no particular attachment to that gentleman, about whom they knew little and cared less. Except in places like public schools, where the house is an identifiable unit, those in charge of houses spend a great deal of their time trying to generate enthusiasm for an organization towards which children have no special feelings of allegiance.

The advantage of a horizontal system of pastoral care is that it matches the teaching structure of a secondary school while at the same time lining up with children's natural allegiance to their peers. Every secondary school child is taught in a year group within which particular curriculum and timetable arrangements apply which are different from those of other year groups. Out of lessons, too, children are inclined to go with people of their own age. But these alone are not the reasons why a year system was preferred at Eltham Green in the seventies. House systems have important advantages, not least in training children to get on with those not of their own age and to take responsibility for people younger than themselves. What persuaded me to change was lack of consistency between one house and another. Different standards were applied to people of the same age, depending upon which house they were in. There is no serious problem about first-formers being treated differently from fourth-formers. An eleven-year-old who fails to do his homework is not in the same boat as someone only twelve months away from his public examinations. But it is a different matter if two fourth-formers are reported for being insolent to staff and one is caned while the other gets a relatively friendly reprimand – something that actually happened at Eltham Green when two miscreants were dealt with by two heads of houses with divergent views on discipline. The more one thinks about it, the more unlikely it appears that a school will find eight heads of houses with anything approaching identical views on all the matters they have to deal with. The friction and injustice this creates can become intolerable. With a horizontal structure, the problem disappears. It matters not that the head of third year sees things differently from the head of fourth year: they will each be consistent within their year group, which is all that justice requires and children expect.

As long ago as 1776, the economist Adam Smith observed that nations prosper when they recognize that specialization leads to dexterity. Pastoral systems flourish when based upon the same recognition. An important advantage of horizontal structures is that they allow teachers to become specialists. Thus, the head of sixth form becomes an expert in dealing with older pupils; in filling in university application forms; in sorting out the fifth-form recruit who has three CSE passes, two O levels, a bit of something in the way of RSA typing, and a burning ambition to enter RADA. Similarly, the head of first year develops an expertise in handling very small and anxious newcomers (and those not so small and not sufficiently anxious). Special skills are required at every level of a child's development. This is true not only of heads of years but also of form teachers who are in the front line in the provision of pastoral care.

Table 6: The Horizontal Pastoral Structure

→	Sixth Form	Head of Sixth Form and team of Form Teachers have permanent responsibility for the Sixth
↻	Fifth Year .... Fourth Year	Head of Fourth Year and team of Form Teachers move with the year group into the Fifth, subsequently reverting to the Fourth
→	Third Year	Head of Third Year and team of Form Teachers have permanent responsibility for the Third
↻	Second Year .... First Year	Head of First Year and team of Form Teachers move with the year group into the Second Year, subsequently reverting to the First Year

→ Fixed Pastoral Team

↻ Revolving Pastoral Team

Table 6 is a diagramatic representation of how the year system works at Eltham Green. The head of year and team of form teachers who receive a group of newcomers into the school look after them for two years, then drop back to collect a fresh intake. The head of third year is a fixed star in the pastoral firmament: something that derives from my belief that it is in the third year that boys and girls go through the most difficult period in their development and need special handling. This opinion was firmly supported by the commission on discipline whose report was mentioned in chapter two. The third year is also a time of academic transition, when children choose their examination courses for the upper school: an exercise that requires a specialist in charge. On moving into the fourth, pupils are picked up by a head of year and a team of form teachers who stay with them for two years and see them through their first public examinations. The case for their having the same person in charge throughout their preparation for the day of judgement is obvious, as is the reason for having a permanent head of sixth form. Of course, the heads of years and form teachers occasionally yearn for a broader canvas upon which to work. The latter may, in fact, make a request for a change and be moved to a different team at the start of a new school year.

Like most things at Eltham Green, the duties and responsibilities of heads of years and their deputies are set down in writing:

Heads of Years
> General welfare of pupils
> Discipline with heads of departments
> Annual and interim reports
> Year assemblies
> General responsibility for pupils outside lesson times
> Close liaison with form teachers in implementation of school policies

Deputy Heads of Years
> Registers
> Attendance
> Organization of late detentions
> Sharing with heads of years in checking and signing school reports
> Uniform, appearance and discipline of pupils of own sex
> Any other duties delegated by heads of years

These definitions are made necessary by two influences at work. Firstly, heads of years have a natural disinclination to give their deputies any really important jobs to do. This is frustrating for the energetic young teacher who very often gets appointed to a deputy head of year post. The reluctance of pastoral heads to delegate is something every head teacher knows about. Perhaps it arises in part from the fact that those who reach such positions are sometimes not in the top bracket professionally. Unable to obtain promotion to head of department positions on the academic side (which is the normal route to where the power really lies), they are determined to make the most of what authority they possess. 'She is,' claimed one of my heads of years about his young deputy, 'far too young to deal with him.' The reference was to a very difficult father who needed a good straight talk. He got it though, from a young Liverpudlian who handled him better than her superior would have done. The education system is beginning to work its way out of the sort of difficulty described, caused in part by the indiscriminate appointment of mature but ineffectual teachers to senior pastoral positions in reorganized schools. When Eltham Green absorbed several local schools at its formation in 1956, some extraordinary appointments were made with which the school had to live for as much as twenty years.

The second reason why clear definitions of role are necessary, is the traditional tension in a large school between those with senior pastoral posts and those in senior academic appointments: the heads of years *versus* heads of departments problem. Given the chance, heads of years will have a good deal to do with advising children on what to do about their academic problems. But in my view, this ought properly to be referred to those whose responsibility it is to monitor and control academic standards, namely heads of departments. This is not to say that there is never a time for heads of years to be involved in academic decisions. A good deal of what has been said already with regard to the third year and above makes it plain that participation is essential at certain stages. But the burden of effort on the academic side and, more important, the right to decide, must rest with heads of departments. Thus, the head of third year presents a comprehensive list of recommendations as to which pupils should take which courses in the upper school, but it is the heads of departments who determine whether to accept them or not. It is my considered opinion that the line between pastoral and academic responsibility must be as clearly drawn as any of the distinctions that are necessary to the successful operation of a large school.

The general welfare of pupils, for which pastoral heads are responsible, may touch upon any area of their life in and out of school. In the event, heads of years at Eltham Green spend most of their time and energy dealing with matters which it is possible to collect together under the headings how pupils look and behave, problems at home, and progress at school.

HOW PUPILS LOOK AND BEHAVE

Mandy arrived for the new school year with earrings dangling almost to her shoulders. She was soon in the corridor outside my study, together with the usual customers whose appetite for trouble was greater than that for breakfast (a meal they rarely had as it would have required a monumental reorganization of their sleeping habits). Mandy had her explanation about the earrings ready: 'Me dad give 'em to me, 'cos you took me others.' Indeed I did: my one small contribution to the constant battle waged by heads of years against the tide of jewellery, fashion shoes, make-up and other symbols of unorthodoxy which threatens to engulf any comprehensive school. One of the things which astonished me when I first moved into the comprehensive sector was the extraordinary view some girls seemed to have of what made them look attractive. Even more remarkable, was the fact that there were boys who actually responded.

There are those who think that pastoral staff waste too much time on seeing to it that pupils observe school rules about uniform and general appearance. Such people miss the point of it all. The scriptures tell us that those who are faithful in little will be faithful in much. Almost invariably, a youngster who is being awkward about what to wear to school is awkward about a great many other things as well, like how hard he works and how he speaks to teachers. I never cease to be amazed at the gullibility of parents who allow themselves to be dragged in on the wrong side of this argument and encouraged to support their wayward offspring. 'If your teachers', wrote one irate mother, 'spent more time teaching properly and stopped getting on to my Debbie, they would be doing what they are supposed to be there for. If there's any more of it, I'm coming up.' And come up she eventually did, to reclaim the nine bracelets, seven rings, four necklaces, three sets of earrings and one pair of platform shoes we had confiscated. Face to face, she admitted Debbie was a bit of a handful. 'She's a right cow at home, I can tell you.' But it would all be different from now on. It was a wonderful school with lovely teachers and they were doing a fine job. Never again would Debbie be allowed to come to school other than properly dressed with no jewellery. Mother would check each morning for signs of mascara, lipstick and nail varnish – 'specially that green she wears' – before sending her off to school. It didn't happen, of course. Debbie's parents had surrendered their authority long before.

Another favourite tactic of parents in defence of their malattired offspring is the approach that goes, 'I've stood outside your school gates and seen lots of them coming out worse than our Tommy. You're picking on him.' This is most frequently used by parents who do not like our school rule about boys not having their hair below the collar. They know what the rule is, of course, and have indicated their assent to it when accepting a place. The explanation that our failure to spot some defaulters does not mean we should ignore the rest carries little weight with these passionate defenders of justice. 'I still say you're picking on him.' Every pastoral head has heard parents use the same argument when a youngster is brought before a court for burglary.

In the early seventies, when it was not possible to discern the sex of young people if they were walking away from you, heads of years fought a daily battle over the length of boys' hair. One case, which attracted wide media publicity, epitomized the situation. Greg Jenkins was just fourteen when he decided that he was not going to observe the school rule. A guitar-playing youth from the Blackheath area, with no father in evidence to take him in hand, he quickly converted mother to his point of view despite her initial agreement with school policy. Put out of school for refusing to conform, he set about getting himself the maximum publicity. The *Evening News* was first with the story, picturing the boy looking forlorn but determined outside the school gate under the headline 'Greg misses School to save his Locks'. It read:

> Schoolboy Greg Jenkins, aged fourteen, has a shoulder-length problem and so far it has cost him four weeks schooling. His long, flowing, blonde tresses reaching well down his back, are the envy of his school friends, the delight of his girlfriend, and the bane of his headmaster.

Unfortunately, the accompanying photograph was not sharp enough to highlight the lice in Greg's hair. It might perhaps have altered the import of the story. I published the following statement for the information of staff shortly afterwards:

> Colleagues who have been following the Greg Jenkins saga will wish to know that his hair has now been officially declared clean of a particularly virulent type of super-nit. He was deloused at a medical centre in Plumstead the day after his picture was taken for press publication. I would like to use this sorry incident to draw the attention of all staff to the need for keeping an eye on the state of pupil's hair.

Greg wrote to a magazine called *Children's Rights* about the unreasonableness of his headmaster. 'I like my hair long,' he wrote, 'and I see no reason why there should be a ruling about hair.' The magazine agreed with him: they would refer the case to the National Council for Civil Liberties. No one in the media seemed very concerned about the rights of ordinary children who were expected to sit beside the likes of Greg in class.

The boy spent more than six months without education before the education authority organized a place for him at a school that did not have our rule about length of hair. Was I exceeding my powers in refusing to have him back? In 1953, Lord Chief Justice Goddard ruled that questions of dress and appearance in schools were 'a matter of discipline, and a matter which must be within the competence of the headmaster or headmistress of any school, whether it is one of the great public schools, or a county secondary school, or a county primary school. There must be somebody to keep discipline, and of course that person is the head.'

A fitting epilogue to the Greg Jenkins story is that, a few months after he started at his new school, the Principal School Medical Officer of the Inner London Education Authority issued a letter about *pediculus humanus capitis*: the louse which was infesting the heads of growing numbers of London school children. 'It is very easy', it said, 'to catch lice from other people.'

Seeing to it that the Greg Jenkinses and the Debbies and the Mandys don't get away with it is an important part of the work of a head of year, and a time-consuming exercise. But if the battle about dress and appearance is lost, the war is over before the important campaigns about behaviour have even begun. If boys and girls cannot be brought to observe rules about how to present themselves for school, they are hardly likely to worry about how to behave towards staff and other pupils. 'I have confiscated enough platform shoes to open a shoe shop,' said one deputy head of year in the days when wearing platforms was the height of female fashion. Significantly, the general standard of behaviour in that deputy's year group was of a high order.

The head of sixth form is by no means relieved of responsibility for dress and appearance, although school uniform is not worn by members of the sixth. Here is an extract from a letter that goes out in August every year to those who might be thinking about entering the sixth form:

While school uniform is not required, there are a few simple principles which we like observed. Firstly, a few words about the boys. They are expected to wear a collar and tie or a polo neck jumper. T-shirts are not acceptable. An ordinary jacket should be worn, that is to say not a leather one or a jerkin. Jeans should not be worn to school, nor any of the current fashions in denim wear. While hair may be worn quite long, there is a limit which is the top of the collar. If it extends beyond that, then the young man concerned will be sent for a haircut at once. There are just one or two things to be said about girls entering the Sixth Form. Firstly – as for the boys – jeans and denim wear are not acceptable. In more general terms, girls are asked to dress ordinarily and to avoid fashionable extremes. Of course, I realize that setting down principles as to what young people should not wear or how long they may have their hair raises some hackles. I must be frank and say that I am not at all disturbed by that. I believe that parents in general appreciate the need for moderation in the way young people present themselves at school. We have to guard carefully the picture we present to those outside the school. For that reason, anyone whose appearance falls short of the standard described above will not be accepted in the Sixth Form.

We do not draw any moralistic comparisons between modes of dress and social attitudes. Generally speaking, young people of seventeen and eighteen are not very interested in that line of approach. Their own concepts are less sophisticated than older people sometimes think, and they prefer straight talk. The following statement by Helen MacRae in the magazine *Nova* in the autumn of 1972 is pertinent:

Someone once told me that if I wore pink socks to school I wouldn't be able to concentrate on my Latin. They drew the most ridiculous parallels. We were ticked off for leaving greasy chip papers around and were told that, if we did that sort of thing now, when we got to university we would sleep with so many blokes. If they'd just said it was nasty to leave greasy papers around we'd have taken some notice, but they made it into a big moral thing.

Of course, within any year system, different pastoral heads establish their standards in different ways. One of the virtues of that particular method of organization is that it allows the individual to proceed in his own way without any injustice to pupils. Thus the behaviour style of each year group is a reflection of the personality of the year head and his deputy. This is a logical extension of Professor Michael Rutter's thesis. If it is true that what matters for a school as a whole is that it should have a recognizable ethos, it is equally the case that, within a year system, a year group should have its own character. One in which known standards are consistently applied will be happier and more successful than one in which it is not clear what is supposed to be going on. In short, the same judgement applies as to a school as a whole. The position of the pastoral head is therefore a very powerful one indeed. In a large organization, his is a school within a school. It is perhaps a sort of natural justice that he is in a far stronger position to affect the overall ethos of a school than the departmental head, whose route to ultimate authority may be more obvious.

PROBLEMS AT HOME

The pastoral head finds himself cast in many roles. He is a mixture of parent, judge, friend, counsellor and executioner. 'I think', said one of my heads of years after a particularly difficult term, 'I will declare myself insane and find some quiet sanatorium in which to end my days in peace.' Events had reached a climax when the father of one of our girls had come up to attack him for paying too much attention to what mother wanted for their daughter Linda. Both parents were living with people they were not married to but who also wanted a finger in the educational pie as far as Linda was concerned. Whereas mother's boyfriend agreed with her, father's girlfriend disagreed with him, which made him very aggressive. Having two women against him was too much. In the end, the poor head of year was faced with four adults all arguing with one another and wanting him to sort it all out. That quiet sanatorium must have seemed very inviting.

The biggest single influence on a child's school performance is the situation at home. This is true at all levels of ability and applies to every social group. It needs to be emphasized, because some of those who nod their heads at the assertion simply mean that troublemakers come from bad homes. There is far more to it than that. Many good homes are not good enough. A great many parents show just sufficient interest in their children for everything to work out reasonably well. But with greater involvement much more could be achieved. A child's success at school correlates directly with the influence of two groups of people: his teachers and his parents. And the greatest of these is his parents. There are, of course, exceptional children who overcome parental neglect and do wondrous things; but they are extraordinary people. The performance in school of the average, ordinary child rises and falls in direct relation to the amount of interest and concern shown at home.

Parent power is one of the two most important factors at work in the education system. I use that term here in a way in which it is not normally employed, to mean the ability of parents to affect the performance of their own children in school. If mums and dads only knew what a difference they can make, they would be less ready to shake their heads and worry about what is shown on the television and that sort of thing.

Sharing a platform with Mary Whitehouse in the autumn of 1979, I was asked what parents could do to offset the morally corrupting influences at work in our society. The answer is simple: everything. Parents have it all going for them. They provide the primary atmosphere within which boys and girls grow up; they have opportunities for social intercourse every day. No other body of people or organization has such power. The trouble is, many neglect to use it. They decline to talk to their children, go out with them, keep track of their activities and show that continuing, determined, relentless, unending concern for them that is the most awesome responsibility of parenthood. 'We don't have much to do with him these days,' said the parents of one fourteen-year-old boy, 'we let him go his own way.' Broad is the road to destruction, and some parents are inclined to widen the tarmac for their offspring.

It is almost invariably the pastoral head at school who feels the backlash when parents come to their senses. Simon was a boy whose parents persistently failed to respond to requests to come and talk over his problems. Letters were as often as not ignored, although from time to time there was a brief note promising to contact the school next week or at some such time in the future. A more lengthy correspondence developed as Simon's behaviour became more objectionable and moved on from fooling about to theft and violence. 'Look at me,' he was screaming to his parents, 'I'm alive.' Realizing their mistake, they did what many such parents do and took up the cudgels on behalf of their maligned son. 'There are', wrote mother to the boy's long suffering head of year, 'some very undesirable boys at your school and I don't want our Simon tarred with that brush.' Anyone who has held pastoral responsibility in a large school will have lost count of the number of times they have heard that old argument. The first line of defence used by neglectful parents is that their child has been led astray by undesirables from bad homes. Significantly, when Simon's mother and father were finally got to school (after he had been arrested by the police for burglary), they blandly disclaimed all knowledge of most of the letters we had written. They suggested Simon must have intercepted them: he had grown up into that sort of boy, though they couldn't understand why.

There is not a great deal a pastoral head can do when faced with this sort of situation. It would be nice to think he could take the place of the inadequate parent and become an adequate substitute. Many splendid teachers attempt to do just that, but the amount of success is usually very slight. Paradoxically (and how full of paradoxes are those things that bear upon human relationships), the likelihood of achieving something is sometimes greater in the case of a broken home. The mother who has no male support will often welcome the close involvement of a masculine figure at school in the upbringing of her children. But support has to be offered most circumspectly, since such parents are usually very sensitive about their situation, frequently guiltridden, and as often as not even more on the defensive than Simon's were. When the Bible says we should bear one another's burdens, it might well have been addressing its message to the pastoral head of a large comprehensive school.

Part of the burden-bearing means assuming responsibility for children out of school hours. The community at large wants and expects schools to do this, although there are those who seek to question the rightness of it. In the summer of 1977, Eltham Green came under attack from Roland Moyle, the Member of Parliament for Lewisham East, when a boy was punished for bringing the name of the school into disrepute by his behaviour in a Lewisham shop. He was in company with two other Eltham Green boys, one of whom was caught attempting to steal. Since it happened on a Saturday, and the boys were not in school uniform, the parents took the view that the school had exceeded its authority. But, of course, one of the first things the shopkeeper and the police wanted to know was which school the boys came from. There was no way in which Eltham Green could remain unaffected by what had occurred. As usual, the *Evening News* was first into the ring with the headline 'Caning went too far Minister tells Head'. The report said:

> Schoolboy John Smith has been caned for being with a friend who tried to steal from a shop on a Saturday morning. Now his MP, junior health minister Mr Roland Moyle, has accused ILEA and John's Eltham Green comprehensive school of exceeding their authority. The row centres on who is responsible for pupils out of school hours. Mr Moyle, Labour member for Lewisham East, said: 'The boy's parents take the view that once their son is out of school hours, disciplining and regulating his conduct is a matter for them. I share that view.'

The Education Officer for the ILEA gave what can only be described as unqualified support to the school, and that was the end of the matter, notwithstanding threats of legal action by the parents. But the MP who chose to become involved had raised an interesting question that became the subject of a considerable correspondence. One piece of evidence I offered to support the view that ordinary citizens wanted schools to monitor and control the behaviour of children out of school hours was a letter I received at the time of the John Smith affair from someone living near the school. Here is an extract:

> I am writing to you in despair, hoping you can do something to help solve a problem, partially caused by one of your pupils. He is a boy about 15-16 years of age . . . Many times he has, with his friends, harassed the elderly people in this road, and when we try to reason with them, we get ignored or rude remarks. On Monday last they started their capers just after 8 p.m. I went out and asked them quite civilly to move along or go to the park. I was completely ignored and the noise and shouting continued. Further to this, I told them if they persisted to be a nuisance I would call the police, to which they started ranting 'Rah Rah Rah the police are coming' and hand clapping with more ranting. My husband has had two cerebral haemorrhages and is severely paralysed, and suffers from acute headaches, I myself have a heart condition, and the lady opposite has recently returned from hospital after surviving a second heart attack. We are not blaming the boys for our disability, but after working a lifetime, and bringing up a family as decently as we could, we cannot see why we should be subject to such attitudes from the younger generation . . .

It was a cry for help that would be echoed by many old people who are mystified by what the affluent society has done to the manners of young people. The villain was caught and dealt with, and his parents seen by the head of year concerned, who afterwards told me that both mother and father were horrified by their son's behaviour. 'We never knew he was like that,' was their response. Bringing parents face to face with unpleasant reality is another of the responsibilities of a pastoral head.

PROGRESS AT SCHOOL

Despite what has been said before about the heads of years *versus* heads of departments problem, it is clearly necessary for those with pastoral responsibility to be involved in reporting academic progress to parents. In the final analysis, it is the person with pastoral responsibility who has a total view of the situation. Thus, it is he who collates the assessments of effort that go out once a term for each pupil at Eltham Green, and it is he who provides the final summary comment on each pupil's annual report.

I sometimes feel that the education system in general and the Inner London Education Authority in particular owe a debt of gratitude to a group of teachers at Eltham Green who perceived that school reports would be significantly more worthwhile and infinitely more accurate if each subject teacher was, at the time of writing his comments, unaware of what the other subject teachers had written. As with our red card system, which is merely a refinement of every school's daily report system, it's not what you do but the way that you do it that counts.

When at the beginning of the seventies the heads of departments at Eltham Green were expressing dissatisfaction with the traditional form of annual report, a small committee came up with what was then a new idea: one that numerous schools have since written to me about and subsequently copied. In essence, it was simplicity itself. Each department was provided with a supply of tear-off pads, so that the traditional one-page school report was replaced by a booklet containing one page for each subject and a summary page written by the appropriate head of year. Finally, there was a returnable blank page for parents to write their comments. After all the subject pages had been written, they were stacked in sets, one for each pupil, the summary and parental response pages added, and then the whole collection stapled together.

When I was a probationer teacher, I was not sure what to say about some of the pupils I taught. When writing reports, I would look at what the others had written. There was one teacher whose expertise amazed me: he claimed never to have written more than two words on any one pupil, and never to have said anything that was not a variant of the term satisfactory. Thus one pupil was unsatisfactory, while a second was quite unsatisfactory and a third totally satisfactory or even, when the teacher had a rush of blood to the head, tremendously satisfactory. It was remarkable. It was also a farce.

Not being able to see what others have written completely alters the conditions under which the exercise is carried out. The effect is to turn every child's report into a comment upon his teachers as well as his own performance. If eleven of them say what a well-behaved, industrious pupil he is, while a twelfth observes that he is bored and listless, that says a good deal more than the writer intended, does it not? The task of the pastoral head who has to provide an overall summary is made extremely difficult by such a system, but the lengthy business of providing reports becomes a most productive exercise.

Termly assessments are the other means by which progress is reported to parents. These are specifically concentrated not on what children have achieved but upon the amount of effort they have made. A four-point scale from A to D is used: a method which compels a teacher to make up his mind whether a child is working hard (A or B) or not working hard (C or D). Give teachers a five-point scale, and they will avoid committing themselves by using the middle of the scale for most pupils. The assessments are sent to parents, and those pupils with bad ones are brought before a tribunal made up of the director of studies, the senior year master and the head of year concerned. There is no doubt that parents approve of the regularity with which effort is assessed, and the element of drama that we attach to the exercise.

But it would be idle to pretend that such a system is precise in its workings. Teachers find it extremely difficult to distinguish between effort and achievement. Heads of department are good at it; so are remedial specialists. But the ordinary classroom practitioner frequently takes good marks as a sign that a child is working well and bad marks as evidence of the opposite. The reason we first introduced assessments at Eltham Green was to try and identify the boys and girls in the middle of the pack who were coasting along with average marks and not doing justice to their abilities. I do not believe that we have yet developed an effective technique for sorting out this problem. Perhaps it cannot be done through any formalized assessment procedure. There is a certain danger in devising bigger and better systems for monitoring progress. One can end up with no more than a great many sheets of paper decorated with marks that don't mean very much to anybody. This is something that needs to be borne in mind if as a nation we are going in for more extensive assessment programmes.

Before leaving the subject of how pastoral heads spend most of their time, it perhaps needs to be said that their priorities are not always those they would choose if given the opportunity. For example, in my experience many would like to devote less energy to enforcing school uniform rules and more time to liaison with their staff teams. But for much of the time pastoral headship is a matter of responding to events rather than directing them. For that reason, it can be thoroughly demoralizing, and it is one of the most difficult responsibilities within any large comprehensive school.

In dealing with pupils who have problems, heads of years are heavily dependent upon the work of many other professional groups. The growth of large comprehensive schools with carefully structured pastoral systems has in no way diminished the role of those in other services providing support for children in trouble or need. To some extent, the development of large units has introduced new difficulties. People like education welfare officers find themselves dealing with complex organizations with which it is not easy to establish close liaison and mutual understanding.

One comment made at a meeting we had about how to improve communication was, 'I used to know which teacher to ask for when I first went into a school. It was always someone like the deputy head. Nowadays, it could be any one of a dozen people, depending on which child I've come about. If I need to discuss several, it's very confusing. I seem to spend a good deal of my time trying to make contact with the right members of staff at your end of things.' It was a revealing comment, not least because the last statement is exactly what pastoral staff in schools say about the support services.

Establishing who is supposed to be doing what is problem enough in the internal organization of a large school. When external services are included in the scheme of things, the attempt to keep track of what is going on presents an immense challenge. Indeed, the assumption that sense can be made of it seems on occasions to be an optimistic one. Fortunately it does not always matter. I recollect an occasion when a head of year, a welfare officer and a social worker each independently found clothing for a needy family whose house had caught fire. Some weeks later, the parents visited the school to express their thanks that everyone had worked together to provide for them and their children: their three boys had never been so well clothed before. I nodded sagely, not wishing to destroy their simple belief that it had all been carefully organized. Schools, like governments, depend heavily on the fact that those outside the line of action discern pattern and order where sometimes there is none. Emmett John Hughes, writing of one of the more chaotic periods during the Eisenhower administration of the fifties in America, says that 'at the end of a day of administrative disorder, there was an almost tonic effect in reading, in the evening's news columns, a most tidily organized account of all that had happened'. (*The Ordeal of Power*)

It is inevitable that, where there exist several professional groups working in the same field, communication and identity of purpose will not always be readily achieved. It is unrealistic to suppose that agreement between teachers, welfare officers, social workers and the rest will be possible in all circumstances. Even the simplest account of what each is supposed to do makes that clear.

A full analysis of the functions of the different support services as they relate to children is a task for an expert outside the school situation who has a wider knowledge and more objectivity than I possess. What follows is no more than a statement of what *appears* from *inside* a school to be the function of each support group. Details are deliberately brief, since this is an attempt to identify the special contribution and emphasis that seems to be the preserve of each service. The school is taken first as a point of reference.

School Pastoral Structure
To serve closely the interests of pupils who need extra support, but within a framework that takes account of the needs of the majority.

Education Welfare Service
To assist children and the families from which they come in cases of material need, social distress or educational difficulty, especially when school attendance is affected.

Social Services Department
To be concerned for children when there are difficulties at home; when their behaviour or associations place them at risk; when they have been made subject to supervision.

Police
To advise children when their behaviour is likely to lead them into trouble with the law and to counsel their parents accordingly; to arrest children and bring legal proceedings when they break the law.

Juvenile Magistrates
To apply the law within the framework of the Children and Young Persons Act with a view to persuading young people not to behave in ways that bring them into conflict with it.

Educational Psychologists
To see children and their parents when a school feels that a child's difficulties may have psychological causes; to refer children for psychiatric treatment at child guidance centres; to recommend home tuition and placements at other than ordinary schools.

Child Psychiatrists
To provide treatment at child guidance centres; to recommend home tuition and placements at other than ordinary schools.

The list does not, of course, include all the people who assist the development of children in need of help. In churches, youth clubs, uniformed organizations and activity groups of all kinds, there are people establishing important relationships with youngsters who have problems of one kind or another. Community relations officers, general practitioners and many others find ways of giving advice and support. All this provides a backdrop to the work of the professional groups whose functions have been described. These functions overlap and sometimes conflict with one another; some of them are also well-nigh impossible to fulfil. Some illustrations will serve to underline these points. It needs to be borne in mind that these are intended specifically to highlight difficulties rather than demonstrate what is normal.

The concern of the school to maintain an overall style and ethos that is beneficial to the pupil body as a whole raises problems when it comes to dealing with individual casualties. Steve did not like his lessons, did not like his teachers, did not like school and refused to attend. Persuaded after many home visits and much cajolery on the part of the education welfare officer to come to school, he was immediately in trouble for having no uniform and for wearing earrings and boots. The welfare officer rang to ask whether we couldn't forgo our insistence on uniform in this particularly difficult case. Our answer was that we could not allow one pupil to be given that sort of privilege; especially a boy who was likely to go round the school boasting of his ability to beat the system. I am not suggesting there is any right or wrong in a case such as this, but merely that there is an inevitable conflict between what the welfare side is supposed to do (get the child into school at all costs) and what the school is concerned about (preserving the standards for which it has fought hard and long).

When it comes to social workers, they sometimes seem to

regard themselves as the advocates and defenders of the miscreant in face of the establishment as it is represented by the school. There was to be a case conference about Philip's truancy but, since it was hoped the boy would bestir himself sufficiently to attend, it was scheduled for the middle of the day as, according to his social worker, he didn't get up until about then. Such a proposal was like a red rag to a bull to my senior master who had spent hours on the case at the expense of other pupils. The sympathies of the social worker and the school lay in quite different directions precisely because of their different functions.

The implications of the Children and Young Persons Act for the work of police and juvenile magistrates has received enough public attention for a detailed analysis to be unnecessary here. The inability of the legal system to take any kind of effective action against wrongdoers has made lawbreaking a relatively safe activity for young people. The assumption that placing offenders under the supervision of social workers will change their behaviour has been clearly demonstrated as false. The age, inexperience and lack of qualifications of many of those called upon to carry out supervision orders mean they are putty in the hands of the hardened sixteen-year-old troublemaker. 'I have not', said one young social worker given charge of a pupil of mine, 'the slightest idea how to handle him – he terrifies me.' She was a pleasant girl in her early twenties. The boy committed his next offence just two days after being placed under her supervision. It was his eleventh. He was fined ten pounds and his supervision order extended by six months. When he left the court, he was smiling.

The establishment in 1980 of two detention centres with what the Home Secretary calls vigorous régimes will not affect the vast majority of juvenile offenders. Not until a boy has reached the age of fourteen will he qualify for the treatment available at the junior centre in Surrey, and not until he is seventeen will he be considered for the senior one in West Yorkshire. It is therefore clear that the same problem applies as bedevils the work of the support services in general: those young people who get the treatment will very likely already have reached the point of no return. This is not to say that the establishment of strict-régime centres is not a step in the right direction; but they will achieve little unless more is done earlier on in the development of the young offender.

Most teachers would be hard put to it to say accurately what an educational psychologist is supposed to do. They would be inclined to offer a definition more applicable to a psychiatrist. Parents have the same problem, and automatically assume, when one suggests a child should be referred for diagnosis to the former, that it means treatment by the latter. Perhaps the confusion is understandable, since in my experience there are differences of opinion between the two as to what role each should be playing. The commonest result of having both professions involved in treating problem children is that of delay. It took many months for us to get Tony through the hands of the psychologist into those of the psychiatrist. When at the end of it all the boy failed to keep his first appointment at the child guidance clinic, his treatment was cancelled. We were told, 'The psychiatrist does not feel there is much likelihood of someone who failed to keep his first appointment making a meaningful contact with the clinic for the ongoing psychiatric help which has been requested.' Would that the school had been able to dismiss the problems Tony presented in such a swift and decisive manner.

But then, it must be admitted that those working in the psychological and child guidance fields have a good deal to put up with from schools. As often as not, a child who is referred for diagnosis and treatment has nothing wrong with him except a limitless capacity for being a thundering nuisance. Such youngsters are not disturbed, unbalanced, maladjusted or even particularly unhappy. They have simply decided to live their school lives in the style of troublemakers. One goes through the rigmarole of referral and treatment simply in order to mark off one more set of options that have been tried and failed before getting rid of them. They do not, of course, take the treatment seriously; and quite often their parents don't either. 'I know what's wrong with him,' said one father, 'and taking him down the guidance won't help – he's just a right little bleeder like I was at school.' Of course, some children who adopt troublemaking as a way of life do have profound psychological problems and need professional help of an appropriate kind. But there are many others who just take the system for a ride.

Martin was a child who failed to receive all the help that should have come his way. He almost did not come to Eltham Green School. It was clear from his primary school records that, because of learning and behaviour problems, a special school placement should be considered, and I wrote various letters recommending this. However, his parents resisted, and we did our best for him for four years until his suspension became necessary for everyone else's sanity and survival. When nothing was done about providing for him after we had put him out of school, I wrote to the assistant education officer in the special education branch expressing disquiet. His reply held rich promise of what might have been. It was clear from the boy's papers that placement in a school for the maladjusted should have been arranged years before. Any parental resistance could have been overcome by counselling from the inspectorate. Now it was too late and, to make matters worse, while Martin had been declared in need of a home tutor, it had not proved possible to recruit anyone to teach him. The best that could be provided was some help at a centre for dyslexics. It was, the officer felt, 'a poor substitute for the special education he might have enjoyed'. Of course, Martin got into trouble with the law after he left us, and the last piece of news we had of him gave us a smile when it appeared in a local newspaper. He had fallen into the hands of a young social worker who had allowed him to help in servicing his car. To show goodwill, he left the boy in charge of the vehicle, at which point Martin drove off in it.

Whose fault was it that Martin did not receive the special education he needed? Should the school have pressed harder for it at the time of his admission and subsequently? Was the educational psychologist, a key figure in the recognition of maladjustment, less perceptive than she might have been? Should the inspector who authorized his placement in an ordinary school have reviewed the situation afterwards? Or was the whole thing the fault of the parents? It is a sobering thought that Martin would have been more appropriately provided for had the school lost control of him sooner. In short, he was not a big enough disaster at a sufficiently early age.

This gives us the key to understanding a fundamental problem within our present system of provision for children who need more support than the rest: the existing organization is such that help often becomes available only when it is too late to be of much use. There is not a head teacher, welfare officer, social worker, magistrate, policeman or any other such person who would refute that. The great majority of those young people who absorb the attention of the support services are already beyond redemption.

I once heard a head teacher bewailing the fact that a particular pupil was beyond control in class. There was no hope for him in the ordinary school setting; but no one would do anything at this stage. Yet another case of a child being left without support until too late? Not knowing the speaker, I asked a colleague who she was and discovered she ran a local infants school. Those boys and girls who are going to present serious problems in their teens are invariably identified during their primary education. But, since their ability to play truant, bully, disrupt, steal and all the rest of it does not reach dramatic proportions until they have become physically large and have learned cunning from experience, action is deferred.

The inclination to wait until later before doing anything is attributable to two principal influences. Firstly, because of scarce resources, those working in the support services live by hoping for the best with the youngest children and spending what time, energy and placements they possess on those who are a long way down the road to perdition. Secondly, there is what might be called the give-them-a-fresh-start philosophy: an optimistic *credo* based on the belief that a classroom leopard may change its spots when transferred to a different part of the school jungle. To be effective, this view of the world requires that a school be told as little as possible about any child it receives. Political and administrative pressure to that end has been exerted throughout the seventies and will grow in the eighties. The Inner London Education Authority, which is not by any means alone in this, has shown itself extremely reluctant to release the full papers on any problem child until after a school has agreed to take him on. Thus it may not become clear to a head teacher that he is assuming responsibility for someone who should be in a special school until he is on the roll. The view taken by administrators is that it is not up to head teachers to decide who is and who is not in need of special schooling. That position is essential to the bureaucracy given (a) limited resources and (b) lack of agreement between those working in schools and the other professional groups involved in identifying special needs.

As far as institutionalized provision for children who cannot for one reason or another be contained or provided for in ordinary schools, there were two important developments in the seventies, both mentioned in the previous chapter: the Warnock Report and the support centre movement. Both arose from dissatisfaction with existing styles of provision. Indeed, the rapid growth of support centres anticipated the recommendations of Mary Warnock's committee. This did not happen through access to the minds of its members, but as what the Americans call a spasm response to an existing situation.

By June 1976, two years after the Warnock Committee first met (September 1974) and about the same amount of time before its recommendations were published (May 1978), two things had already become clear to the Department of Education and Science. Firstly, that the question of how to provide for children with problems who did not qualify for special education was one requiring urgent attention. Secondly, that schools and local education authorities were taking initiatives that warranted investigation. As a result, the Secretary of State convened a conference in the summer of 1976 'to discuss with representatives of local authority and teacher associations and other interested bodies the problems of non-attendance and disruptive behaviour in schools'. It was agreed that there would be a survey by Her Majesty's Inspectors of 'special units for disruptive pupils in ordinary schools, excluding those provided through special education procedures'.

Significantly, 1976 was the year in which the head teachers in Greenwich decided to pool resources and set up their own support centre for just such pupils. They had by that stage become disenchanted with and slightly desperate about the procedures for placement in any sort of place other than one they themselves controlled. The local educational guidance centre, which was under the control of the schools psychological service, was regarded by a number of head teachers with suspicion. Its function was the provision of short-stay support for children presenting behaviour problems: they were to return to their previous schools after a period of behaviour modification. However, it was extremely difficult to achieve a placement, and children often seemed to come back much worse than when they went: the result of a régime that operated on almost exactly the opposite lines to that which head teachers thought appropriate. Freedom and self-determination appeared to be the basis of operations, whereas schools were looking for a place where disruptives would have a corrective experience in a tightly controlled atmosphere. The same applied to an intermediate treatment centre later established under the control of the social services department. The decision of the Inner London Education Authority to allow the twenty or so head teachers of Greenwich to go it alone demonstrated a trust borne of desperation. If the twin desires to eliminate corporal punishment and reduce suspensions were to have any prospect of coming to pass, it was politically essential that something be seen to be done to meet the problem of the disruptive pupil. By the end of the seventies, Inner London's commitment in this direction was expressed in an annual budget of £2½ millions devoted to its disruptive pupils scheme. But in 1976, things had not reached that stage.

The Greenwich Education Support Centre, initially managed exclusively by local comprehensive heads and run by staff of their choosing, was established with a view to providing a strict régime that pupils would find an unacceptable alternative to knuckling down at ordinary school. Pupils work in individual study carrels and have, during the time of their placement, to produce a file of work to present when returning to where they came from. Parents are required to attend for interview before a child's period at the centre commences, and are called up to acknowledge and accept its ethos. 'It's like a prison over there,' said one father to me. I thought he was going to be difficult, but no. 'It's just what she needs,' he added. In its first three years, the centre achieved an eighty per cent success rate in keeping children within the normal education system. Some parents have offered the teacher-in-charge money to keep their children there.

If the centre sounds as if it has a repressive style about it, that is both true and false. The repression of destructiveness is in my view no bad thing. But in other respects, the boys and girls who go there rediscover their own abilities and blossom. They find a new freedom from their own worst instincts that allows them to grow as they have not done for years. Trapped in a cycle of disruptive behaviour in their normal schools, and called upon to perpetuate it by their admiring peers, they perform outrageously without necessarily wishing so to do. The support centre environment gives them a last chance to make a fresh start. Significantly, many of those who have a spell at the centre go back there to visit regularly.

Of course, the pressure on staff at such an institution is huge and relentless. This is true not only in terms of supervision but also of teaching and preparation. Table 7, taken from a document entitled *A Day in the Life of a Support Centre*, tells the story. It shows the programme for one member of staff, namely the teacher-in-charge, working with five pupils. Her two assistants have similar programmes, but without the administrative burden as well. It is clear that this kind of work calls for qualities beyond the reach of the average teacher.

When in December 1978 Her Majesty's Inspectors produced the report for which the Secretary of State had called two and a half years earlier, it contained some useful information about the variety of behavioural units that had sprung up in response to local needs. It was perhaps significant that Eric Bolton, the HMI

Table 7: A Day in the Life of a Support Centre: Programme of One Member of Staff

	Period 1	Period 2	Period 3	Period 4	Period 5	Homework
Pupil 1 5th year boy average ability CSE	*Maths* (SMP) Revision for CSE: Shifts	*English* Essay: The Argument	*Physics* Revise two-stroke engines	SRA Tan 14	*Technical Drawing* Orthographic Projection	*Maths* (SMP) Revision: Decimals
Pupil 2 4th year girl above average O level & CSE	*Maths* (SMP) Sine/Cosine	*English* Comprehension and Multiple Choice	*Economic History* Canals and Waterways	SRA Tan 4	*Social Studies* The Family	*English* Essay
Pupil 3 4th year boy average to above O level or CSE	*Maths* Revision of Basics: Decimals	*English* Poetry: Criticism and Writing	*RE* Gambling	SRA Gold 2	*Music* Project Work	*English* Précis
Pupil 4 3rd year boy above average	*Maths* Algebra: Indices	*English* Guided Summary: H.G. Wells	*Economics* Money: Trade and Barter	SRA Tan 2	*Geography* Holland: Land Reclamation	*English* Comprehension
Pupil 5 2nd year boy average	*Maths* Algebra: Simplification	*English* Guided Essay	*RE* Prophets and Priests	SRA Green 5	*Science* Electricity Circuits: Sequence and Parallel	*English* Comprehension
Administration	1 hour approximately interviewing two pupils and co-operating with police		Meals accounts updated	EWO contact re truant	Testing new pupil for reading age	Visit by Head of Year

SMP   Schools Mathematics Project
SRA   Science Research Associates (Reading Scheme)

responsible for it, felt the report was out of date by the time it was published, for the speed of developments had left the inspectorate's investigations a long way behind. Nevertheless, *Behavioural Units* makes interesting reading. As it was concerned with both internal sanctuaries and off-site centres, its sweep was broad. In all, there were 239 units providing places for just short of 4,000 pupils, seventy per cent being of the off-site kind. The great majority of units (83 per cent) had been established in the years 1973 to 1977. Clearly, the seventies had given birth to a new educational creation.

Off-site centres had been established in all kinds of places, including a scout hut, a hospital, a drill hall, an old people's home and a court house. While the last seems appropriate enough, one wonders what the regulars at the old people's home made of it all. The financing had some interesting features: it was reported that one unit was denied a regular allocation of funds on the grounds that it was supposed to be a punitive institution. The majority of the units served pupils of secondary age, the largest concentration coming from those in the fourth and fifth forms. 'Children had been known', the report said, 'to refer themselves.' Two statistics of note were those that showed that 27 per cent of units contained children recommended for special education, and that suspended pupils accounted for 25 per cent of those occupying places.

Two conclusions were drawn that will doubtless have something to do with the way provision for disruptive pupils unfolds in the eighties:

1   Procedures for returning pupils to school were often less well developed than those for referral to the units. There was some evidence that schools were often unwilling to take back particular pupils. Successful return most frequently involved youngsters under the age of 14. There was therefore a case to be made for 'earlier identification and intervention'.

2   For some pupils with chronic difficulties it was 'difficult to envisage a return to school'. The establishment of both short-stay and long-stay units therefore had something to be said for

it. Since long-stay arrangements constituted '*de facto* alternative education' there were questions of reasonable financial and curricular provision to be settled.

What was especially interesting about the second of the two recommendations was its open admission that alternative education outside the ordinary school structure might be appropriate without recourse to traditional special education procedures. This is a most dramatic development in the debate about disruptive pupils, but one which is in no way incompatible with the Warnock Report, which might be seen as pointing in exactly the same direction.

Most children are not affected by the care and support systems described in the latter part of this chapter: those with pastoral responsibility in school meet all their needs. Even at that level, they rarely get into any difficulty, and normally pass through the education system quite smoothly and happily. It is something one needs to remember at a time when solving problems frequently dominates educational thinking. It is all too easy for those working in the caring and supportive agencies, and for teachers whose role it is to liaise with them, to forget that ordinary children without problems constitute the vast majority of the school population.

In the summer of 1975, Monja Danischewsky wrote a salutary letter to *The Times* warning us about concentrating our attention too much on our problems:

As if the human race has not enough troubles to bedevil it, we make things worse by continuing to warn each other of the fatal consequences of our everyday habits. Smoking gives us cancer; butter clogs our arteries; eggs ruin our livers; sweets rot our teeth; coffee gives us insomnia; brandy brings on heart attacks; sex drives us mad; no sex drives us madder – and so on. Could we not rationalize the situation into one all-embracing statement: *Just Living Kills You In The End*? A Government health warning to that effect could be made to appear, by law, on all birth certificates.

The large comprehensive school has succeeded in creating pastoral care systems that meet children's needs far better than they were met in the past. Backing this up are support services which, despite all the problems mentioned, provide an adequate supplement to the efforts of schools on a great many occasions. In consequence, I would guess that well over ninety per cent of the girls and boys going through the education system at any one time are destined to emerge from it as well educated, balanced and mature individuals.

Eight

Governors

During a heated discussion at a meeting of governors in the early seventies, the chairman felt impelled to remind those present of the extent of a headmaster's powers. He quoted the declared policy of the Inner London Education Authority referred to in chapter two: 'The decision as to the conduct of his school in relation to its internal organization and its disciplinary methods is that of the headmaster.' It was an assertion that, like his general support for the traditional view of headship, was to cost him the chairmanship and lead to his resignation from the governing body after something like fifteen years of distinguished service to the school. It was a parting of the ways that foreshadowed dramatic changes in the division of powers between those serving as school governors and those actually working in schools. Increasingly during the seventies, the notion of governors as a group of amateurs giving support to professional people has given way to something quite different. While the head teacher and his staff are still of necessity responsible for running the school in which they earn their living, the function of governors now goes well beyond polite interest in what is going on and is more and more concentrated on examining polices and promoting or obstructing them on political grounds. As an extension of this, the eighties will without doubt witness a growing tendency for governing bodies to act as courts of appeal on a much wider range of issues than in the past.

While the incentive for change comes from new attitudes towards power and influence in the education system, the basis for what is happening was laid a long time ago when local authorities attempted to distinguish in general terms between their own powers and those of the head teachers they might appoint. They were required to do this by the 1944 Education Act, which made it mandatory for every school to be conducted in accordance with articles of government that described the functions to be exercised by the local education authority, the governors and the head teacher. The outcome is well illustrated by the articles of government that apply to all schools run by the Inner London Education Authority. They establish that 'the head teacher shall control the conduct and curriculum, the internal organization, management and discipline of the school, the choice of equipment, books and other resources, the methods of teaching and the general arrangement of teaching groups and shall exercise supervision over the teaching and non-teaching staff.' These terms would seem sufficiently clear and unambiguous to give steely confidence to the most apprehensive recruit to headship. But going along with them is a statement that grows in significance with every increase in political interest in education: 'The Authority shall determine the general educational character of the school and its place in the Authority's educational system. Subject thereto, the governors shall, in consultation with the head teacher, exercise the oversight of the conduct and curriculum of the school.' It would be difficult to contrive a definition of powers more likely to create problems at a time when educational opinion is becoming polarized. While the articles referred to, which are typical of those used by local authorities up and down the land, were good enough in the days when education was less subject to acrimonious political debate, it is unlikely they will see us through the eighties for two principal reasons.

Firstly, there is an obvious conflict between the right of a local authority to determine the educational character of a school and the head teacher's responsibility for its conduct and curriculum. Only when each party refrains from pressing its case too hard will serious problems be avoided. Secondly, the nature and extent of oversight by governors has until now never been properly examined. Educational peace is only to be had if no one asks too many questions about who is supposed to be overseeing what. Once the queries begin, the storm breaks. The desire of the local authority on the one hand and the governors on the other to have more direct and effective influence on what actually happens inside schools on a day-to-day basis has been a feature of the seventies.

But pressure for modification of the head teacher's role has also come from another quarter. When the Inner London Education Authority set up a working-party to examine the internal government of schools, its terms of reference made specific mention of the involvement of assistant teachers in the decision-making process. The subsequent report, published in the spring of 1974, was emphatic about the need for head teachers to consult with their colleagues, to be accessible to them, and to show a readiness to listen to their ideas about the running of their schools. The doctrine of consultation, which dominated the public statements of many local politicians and administrators in the seventies, was offered as a panacea for any number of educational ills. Most particularly, it was seen as the key to problems created by the growth of large comprehensive schools in which the head teacher could not possibly function in the same way as those who had run smaller schools under the old tripartite system. The 1974 working-party was quite clear about the new situation: 'The role of the head has become widely recognized in recent years as a changing one. The context in which a head works is significantly different in many respects from that of only a few years ago. Two major changes of many that can be identified are the increased size of schools and the complexity of the pattern in which many are operating.' The days of the head as a sort of charismatic educational mastermind were clearly numbered. As if to underline just that point, the authors of the report stated that the placing of ultimate responsibility for the running of a school on the shoulders of its head teacher was a situation that was not immutable. It was possible that the day might come when school articles of government might be amended 'to place the balance of responsibility elsewhere'.

A year after the publication of this report, the then Secretary of State for Education and Science, Reg Prentice, set up the Taylor Committee with a brief to review arrangements for the government of schools. Almost half the committee of twenty was made up of local politicians and education officers, thereby reflecting the official view of whose opinions mattered most and where future power should lie. There were but four teachers, and only one of them was an ordinary assistant.

On its publication in September 1977, the Taylor Report reflected the political and administrative interests of its principal authors. Its recommendations were clearly directed towards a reduction in the power and influence of head teachers and a fairly dramatic increase in the control exercised by school governors.

Three paragraphs of the report provide adequate illustration of the committee's intentions for the future control of the individual school as a component of the education system. The first sets the direction; the second drives matters home; the third summarizes a new power structure.

Paragraph 5.29 states that the nature of the relationship between school and parent should be set down in a letter sent by governors to each parent accepting a place at a school. In the past, one of the most important functions of a head teacher has been explaining to parents how communication and co-operation operate and encouraging them to take place. The notion that this process would be better initiated by governors is typical of the new thinking. It is an attempt to place the governing body at the forefront of a school's relationship with parents right at the start of a child's education.

Paragraph 6.23 takes the matter of giving increasing prominence and influence to governors a great deal further. Referring to the curriculum, it states:

> The governing body should be given by the local education authority the responsibility for setting the aims of the school, for considering the means by which they are pursued, for keeping under review the school's progress towards them, and for deciding on action to facilitate such progress.

Such a pattern of gubernatorial responsibility would, of course, be a dramatic departure from the situation that is commonly defined in existing articles of government. It takes the question of oversight of the curriculum far beyond anything envisaged in the past, and transfers responsibility for establishing both curricular aims and methods. Under such a definition of powers, the governing body of a school would be fully entitled to decide which subjects should be taught in the lower part of a secondary school, which examination options should be available higher up, what sort of streaming, setting or ability mixing should be used, and so on. The ramifications are almost endless and give governors the right to determine each and every aspect of the teaching situation.

The response of the National Association of Head Teachers to this particular recommendation has been forthright and unambiguous. While supporting the traditional practice whereby head teachers keep governors informed about the curriculum and its development, it totally rejects the Taylor recommendation on the grounds that governors do not have the competence to set aims and objectives in a field where even the professionals find such exercises complex and immensely difficult. 'No amount of training', says the NAHT, 'will fit governors for this specialized role or give them the understanding of our education system and the necessary expertise to assess progress.' It should remain the responsibility of the head teacher and his staff to 'control and design the curriculum so that it is appropriate for the pupils they serve'.

Paragraph 6.33 provides the final *dénouement*, extending the range of the recommendation on control of the curriculum to cover standards of behaviour as well:

Within the framework of any general policy made by the local education authority, the governing body should have the responsibility for formulating guidelines which promote high standards of behaviour and for making such minimum rules and sanctions as are necessary to maintain such standards in the school.

A governing body possessing such powers would effectively

remove from any head teacher his responsibility for the internal organization, management and discipline of his school. What political nominees might regard as high standards of behaviour would not necessarily coincide with the view of classroom practitioners. Indeed, there is a good deal of evidence to the contrary. The kind of things local councillors get excited about and think important are rarely those that matter most. What is more, their reasons for getting excited about them quite often have more to do with political self-interest than educational philosophy.

It has been argued that the increased powers for governors envisaged in the Taylor Report would not mean an increase in political control because the recommendations about membership of governing bodies would work against that. The proposal that there should be equal numbers of local education authority representatives, school staff, parents and representatives of the local community should, it is argued, ensure a more appropriate range of interests than at present applies. The likelihood is, however, that political people will continue to form the largest group, since it is specifically required that local councillors should be regarded as eligible in two categories: as local education authority nominees and as local community representatives. It is not difficult to see why the politico-bureaucratic axis on the Taylor Committee insisted on that being spelled out. Furthermore, it is to be the responsibility of the local education authority to draw up the list of people to be considered for co-option as community representatives on any governing body. There seems little doubt where the power is intended to lie should the proposals ever be implemented.

The essentially political nature of the intended membership structure is most clearly revealed in a final note that, in compiling its list of possible community representatives, the authority should always invite local trade unions and employers' organizations to make nominations. A whole range of very obvious community interests receive no specific mention, most notably the church and youth organizations. The committee's view of school government as a political activity is plain to see.

Behind the thinking of the Taylor Report is the fear that a governing body might, unless politically weighted, cease to be the agent and partner of the local education authority which carries responsibility in law for the provision of schooling in an area. The fear is not without foundation: conflict between governors and County Hall reached scandalous proportions over the appointment of Dr Rhodes Boyson's successor at Highbury Grove School in the mid-seventies. Perhaps that was in the minds of those who drafted a document sent out to head teachers by the Inner London Education Authority at the beginning of 1978. Entitled *The Powers and Responsibilities of Head Teachers*, it offered a reminder that the head derives his authority from the local education authority and that, in any conflict between governors and County Hall, 'it is with the Authority that the head teacher's accountability must ultimately rest'.

The same document carried at its conclusion an interesting analysis of the head teacher's general executive role:

> He feeds in vision and ideas along with his staff on the one hand; on the other he ensures that appropriate decisions are taken at the right time and that such decisions are effectively implemented. The extent to which the head teacher reserves to himself the power to make decisions may vary somewhat from school to school, but staff views should be sought and decisions made in the light of them. Whatever the process, however, the ultimate responsibility for the decisions rests with the head teacher. He must be prepared to justify decisions taken and accept as his responsibility the consequences that flow from them. The head teacher's role does not, however, stop there. When decisions have been made the head teacher has the executive responsibility for ensuring that they are implemented and that all the staff act in accord with them. The conditions and terms of employment issued with a teacher's letter of appointment by the Authority stipulate that the teacher is required to perform such duties as a member of the staff of a school as shall be entrusted to him by the head teacher.

The statement is an interesting illustration of the point reached towards the end of the seventies in the great debate about power and responsibility in schools. It reiterates the doctrine of consultation while attempting, at the same time, to reassert the traditional right of the head teacher to be obeyed. Whether local education authorities are going to be able to have it both ways is extremely doubtful. Staff consultation and participation are one thing when carried out at the behest of the head teacher in a manner devised by him; they become something quite different when enshrined in some statutory structure carrying the seal of approval of a local authority. It is the latter towards which the education system is moving and which is presented in the Taylor Report. But if the members of staff of a school are led to believe they have a more formalized right to be consulted than in the past, they are not going to be satisfied to go along with what the head decides. It is precisely because of Inner London's experience that it has been found necessary to spell out the head's right to have the last word. But in the end, it will not work. What consultation and participation have come to mean to some teachers during the seventies is the right to have things their way. Thus any decision that goes against them is condemned as having been made without adequate consultation. Not intending to be taken too seriously, one of my heads of department summed things up very nicely after numerous meetings about the perennial problem of examination options. 'Consultation', he said, 'means I'm going to keep everybody talking until I get what I want.' Of course, everyone knows that a really wise, diplomatic, sensitive, astute head teacher will be able to manage the consultation business so that everyone believes things have come out the way they intended. But it becomes ever more difficult as one's colleagues are pressed to regard the head as little more than a general adminstrator whose function is to act upon the advice of those around him.

If the power and influence of staff is to continue to grow, there must be a sharing of responsibility too. The discussion inevitably leads back to the recommendation of the 1974 working-party referred to earlier. Perhaps the eighties will see the placing of ultimate responsibility for the running of a school on shoulders other than those of its head teacher. It is an exciting prospect, for all kinds of reasons.

The most serious threat to the power and authority of the head teacher is not presented by pressure from staff to be consulted but by a growing determination on the part of governors and local authority politicians to take control. The recommendations of the Taylor Report were anticipated in those changed attitudes that brought about the downfall of my first chairman, who knew only the old way of doing things. His resignation was in due course followed by that of others who deplored the political heat generated in the new kind of gubernatorial kitchen. Someone who had, like the chairman, given distinguished service to the school and seen it through its formative years, withdrew on the grounds that governors' meetings had taken on the character of local party ward meetings. A governor who had been a head teacher herself was shouted down for expressing opinions that were not acceptable. I wrote to apologize for the way she had been treated. One sentence of the letter summed up the situation: 'I'm afraid it has to be said the behaviour of our governors would not be tolerated in any classroom in this school.'

These developments serve to illustrate how the way in which a school is run will inevitably change if political influence overrides professional authority. The most vociferous of the local councillors who have exerted themselves at Eltham Green in the seventies have done no more than behave in ways natural to the political animal. They would regard the claim that such methods are out of place in a school as merely showing how out-of-date the education system has become. The nature of the conflict between the old and new ways of running schools is no better illustrated than in the appointment of staff. Here battle is really joined, as one example will show.

In the spring of 1976, four candidates were called for interview for head of history at Eltham Green. They were invited to have lunch and spend some time in the school before being seen by the governors at an evening meeting. After making their acquaintance, I realized that one of them was probably the right man for us while another was almost certainly unsuitable.

Ten governors – about half the total number – attended the meeting at which the appointment was to be made. The chairman was among the absentees, and the chair was taken by a man whose arrival on the governing body had been somewhat unusual: he was appointed soon after making a lengthy complaint to the education authority about my way of running the school. My tactics at the meeting were at best poor and at worst a disaster. Asked at the end of the interviews to make a recommendation, I not only made clear where my choice lay but at the same time explained that one of the candidates was not at all right for the school and should definitely not be appointed. The governors divided 5 to 4 in favour of the person I had specifically urged them not to appoint, there being one abstention. My request that my opposition to the appointment should be minuted was ignored.

Matters could not be left there. Either the candidate who had been appointed had to be persuaded to withdraw, or it was time for me to resign. I am aware that some head teachers now accept it as a matter of course that governors ignore their advice in appointing staff and expect them to suppress their own professional judgement. When I spoke at a training class for newly-appointed school governors, I was told in no uncertain terms that it was not the job of a school teacher to argue the point with elected representatives. In the spring of 1977, an ex-chairman of the Inner London Education Authority made a public attack on me in the press for suggesting in a radio discussion that a particular point of ILEA policy was unsound. It was, he stated, time for me to consider a change of employer. 'There is', he wrote, 'a growing tendency among some elitist educationalists to have little conception of the distinctions between professional advice and opinion and the reality of political decision-making.' The general thrust of this attack was in the same direction as the appointment my governors made against my recommendation. Both raise the same fundamental question: should education be seen as a function of politics, or should the predominant influence in its development be professional? Dame Mary Green, the first headmistress of

Kidbrooke School, summed it up in the fifties when the battle was raging about whether her comprehensive should absorb the local grammar school. Anthony Sampson quotes her in his *Anatomy of Britain* as saying, 'I wish we could keep politics out of it.' That relatively small voice has grown first to a shout and then to something like a scream of anguish in the sixties and seventies as more and more political inroads have been made upon what were once professional preserves. It is now clear that we cannot keep politics out of it. That being so, the head teacher has to learn the art of wheeling and dealing if he is to survive.

Early in the morning after the head of history interviews, I rang the successful candidate and told him that his appointment did not have my support and approval. I said I felt he ought to be made aware of this before selling up his home in the Midlands and moving with his family to London. He responded by expressing his intention to withdraw, which he subsequently did in writing.

There were, of course, considerable repercussions. The governors were angry, but could do nothing. The Chief Inspector for the Inner London Education Authority received a complaint from the candidate's professional association. Matters were brought to a conclusion when the chairman and I were invited to sign documents drawn up by the inspectorate undertaking to do things differently in future. They were of a kind to be interpreted any way one wished, but seemed to satisfy officialdom.

There is an important lesson to be learned from these events. In future, a head teacher will be asking for trouble if he allows anyone whose acceptibility is at all doubtful to reach the final interview stage for a post. It is now a common practice for head teachers to conduct their own preliminary interviews when filling senior positions to ensure that those candidates who eventually come before governors are entirely acceptable. There are three principal results. Firstly, the appointing process has become lengthier and more time-consuming than before. Secondly, marginal candidates are being denied the useful experience of facing governing bodies. Thirdly, short lists have become briefer. 'Were there really only two people worth interviewing?' asked one of my governors when we were seeking a head of department not long ago. An honest answer would have been, 'Actually, there were three or four, and you would have seen all of them if you could be trusted to listen to professional advice.'

Given power over staffing appointments, and the readiness to use it, governors hardly need to have their position strengthened in the ways the Taylor Report envisages. He who controls the troops, controls the direction of the battle. Once a governing body gets it into its head that it will appoint teachers in line with criteria other than those offered by professionals, the future of education moves out of the hands of those trained to provide it. If that is what the nation wishes, so be it. But it is as well to be aware of the direction in which things are moving.

A second important area in which governors have come to exert an increasingly intrusive influence during the seventies concerns school discipline. In general, one can be fairly sure that any firm disciplinary action will be regarded as questionable. In any case of difficulty with parents, support is likely to be at best moderate. The political reasons for this are obvious and understandable, but they make the educational implications no less serious.

Barry Hart was taken on at Eltham Green after a long record of misbehaviour at a neighbouring comprehensive. The headmistress of Barry's school expressed the view that a male head might be able to handle the boy's father more successfully than a female one: a subtle concession to a headmaster's ego that could not fail to succeed. Thus Mr Hart arrived one day for interview with his son and gave every possible undertaking about supporting a hard line with Barry. All went well for an initial period, but then there was a dramatic decline. In his third-year report Barry's teachers variously described him as disturbing, disruptive, uncooperative, hostile and dangerous. The most serious of several misdemeanours took the form of his killing two toads in the science laboratory by pouring chemicals on them. Father's early promises had by this time evaporated, and he had become extremely hostile. He refused to allow his son to make payment for the toads he had killed and went to County Hall to complain about our attitude. The end of the road was reached in the summer of 1976, when Barry was put out of a science laboratory for disruptive behaviour during a lesson about electricity. Knowing what he was capable of, the boy clearly had to be suspended. By now, Mr Hart's hostility had become intense, and he came to the school to express himself in a most threatening manner. Inevitably, he appealed against his son's suspension.

Astonishingly, the appeal was upheld by the vice-chairman of the governors who heard the case on behalf of the governing body. There was an immediate outcry from the staff, who asked that a full meeting of the governors should reconsider the case. We were now into very dangerous waters indeed so far as relationships between the politicians and the professionals were concerned. A confrontation between them was to be avoided at all costs. In any case, Barry Hart could not be allowed to return to Eltham Green to wreak further havoc. The solution lay with the legal eagles at County Hall, who responded to my request that Mr Hart should be warned about his threatening behaviour. They wrote telling him that the Inner London Education Authority would not tolerate its staff being threatened; that legal proceedings might follow any repetition; that he was not in future to enter any part of the Eltham Green premises without the headmaster's prior permission. The local divisional officer rang me to say, 'We've had Mr Hart in here waving a letter at us and asking us to transfer his boy to another school. I suppose you had something to do with that.' Indeed I did.

Handling disciplinary problems of the kind Barry Hart presented is only possible if a school is able to rely on the sympathetic understanding and support of its governors. But such support will not invariably be available. Many school governors now see themselves as the defenders and advocates of those who wish to challenge the professionals. That oversight that it is their duty to exercise is seen in terms of keeping the school's actions in check. Paradoxically, the people most likely to take advantage of this are the least cooperative parents of the most troublesome children. The message is the same as in other areas of educational activity: it is the well-behaved child from the supportive home who seems destined to gain least from the developments that are taking place.

While the two cases which have just been described serve to illustrate how school governors may ignore the advice and usurp the judgement of the head teacher, they leave out of account the other power struggle that is destined to grow in significance: that between governors on the one hand and local education authorities on the other. Some indication of the latter's sensitivity on this subject is provided by the Stephen Price case.

Stephen was formally expelled by the governors of a neighbouring comprehensive school with a record that made Barry Hart look like a model pupil. He was described as being fascinated by fire, had started more than one in school, and was about to appear in court on a charge of setting fire to Her Majesty's mail at the time we were asked to consider him. He had sought an 'unusually close friendship' with another boy and, when his advances were rejected, bullied him. His mother was, according to one official report, 'increasingly apprehensive for her own safety' because of her son's appetite for violence. On one occasion, he had wrapped a window cord round another pupil's neck. There had been referrals to counsellors, psychologists and psychiatrists, but none had brought any improvement in Stephen's behaviour. His expulsion was made with a governor's *caveat* that he should be placed in a special school. The local education authority chose to ignore the *caveat* and transfer the boy to Eltham Green. My protests received a cool adminstrative response. I was directed to take the boy despite his record, and not to tell my governors of his previous history. In short, we were to take on roll a pupil with a psychiatric record and a reputation for fire-raising and violence, but the facts of his case were to be kept from those whose task it was to exercise oversight of the school. Had the implications not been so serious, the situation would have been laughable. And yet, it made legal and administrative sense. It is the responsibility of a local education authority to provide education for every pupil of school age within its administrative area. To that end, every boy and girl must be enrolled at a school. Thus, the power of governors to expel merely solves one problem while creating another. Any boy or girl put out of one school has to be found a place in another. Since some governing bodies are more ready to expel than others, this creates a totally inequitable situation for those schools that try to solve their own problems.

There is one particular sense in which the task of the head teacher is infinitely simpler than that of the authority that employs him: he has only one set of problems to worry about, namely those attaching to his own school. My next move in the Stephen Price case was obvious. I would call the boy for interview, but make it impossible for his parent to accept the placement. My behaviour on her arrival with her son and sister-in-law quickly persuaded Mrs Price that I was not a suitable person to have charge of Stephen. I asked the sister-in-law to keep a close eye on the boy while I talked to his mother, lest he burn the school down. With that for starters, the interview was brief and the conclusion foregone. Mother's subsequent letter of complaint to those who had directed her to me described Eltham Green as a concentration camp. I had clearly got my message across.

It is an old adage that sometimes one has to be cruel to be kind. Stephen Price would in no way benefit from a convenient administrative shuffling of his school placement; special provision was the only possible line of salvation for him. The governors of the school that expelled him had realized that. Significantly, as a result of his rejection by me, the local authority had no alternative but to act upon the *caveat* that had previously been provided by way of advice and guidance.

It would be tedious to spell out all the points that might be made from this case, but one is obvious. If that supervision that governors are expected to exercise over the affairs of a school is to be intensified in the ways envisaged in the Taylor Report, their powers must be increased so that they have authority not only over who may remain at a school but also over who may be admitted. If that does not make sense, logic has gone the way of the dodo. There is no contradiction between this call for an increase in the power of governors and my reservations about the control of schools passing into their hands. In the matter of school government, we are talking about a balance of power no less subtle than that which lies at the heart of the constitutional monarchy within which the English education system operates. How is it that our political system contrives to combine those two apparent opposites, monarchy and parliamentary democracy? At least part of the answer lies in the character and motivation of the people involved. The success of that potentially valuable but extremely volatile partnership which exists between the head teacher of a school, its governing body and the local education authority that built it, depends more than anything else on the sort of people in the situation, especially as far as the first two parties are concerned. Nothing could be worse for the education system in the eighties than an increase in the influence of political school governors; but nothing could be better than the development of more representation and power for parents and teachers.

It is both interesting and revealing to look back on the hesitancy with which the Inner London Education Authority – a proud member of the advance guard – introduced parent and teacher membership of governing bodies. At the outset, in the early seventies, one of each was thought enough for a governing body of twenty. When pressure came for an increase in parental representation, the greatest opposition came from parents already sitting as political nominees. They perceived with absolute clarity that their influence would be significantly diminished by the arrival of elected people who could claim some degree of general parental support. While that was something that could not be pressed too hard in view of voting figures at parent-governor elections, political parents had little enough reason to feel secure. When one of them queried the right of one of my first parent-governors to claim any sort of representative status, he got the dusty answer, 'And just how many people turned out to vote for *you* at the local elections, councillor?'

The prospect of your own child being affected or the progress of your own professional career determined by the decisions made about a school is something that marvellously concentrates the mind on getting things right. Conversely, if what one decides about the curriculum or discipline or deployment of resources has no real and immediate implications for oneself and one's own, the mind may well wander off down the pathway of prejudice to the land of yesterday's-axe-to-grind from whose bourne no educational traveller returns. In short, parent-governors and teacher-governors have to live with what happens in their schools in a way that does not apply to other governors. That being so, their influence should be greatly increased. Without a shadow of doubt, many of the discussions on the governing body at Eltham Green during the seventies would have taken a different turn had a significant number of the teaching staff – enough when allied with parents to match the voting power of political interests – been there. What is more, the headmaster might have been subject to rather more informed questioning and had his inadequacies more clearly demonstrated. That needs saying, lest anyone should think that the development of a strong parent/teacher axis on a governing body necessarily means buttressing the head's authority. The opposite might well be the case; but it would be a step in the right direction for all that. It would be hard to imagine a group of governors more likely to make sound decisions than one containing half a dozen of the most successful teachers in a school and half a dozen of the most supportive parents. This is not to say there should not be a body of other representatives to provide balance and an objective view. If one borrows from the Taylor Report the idea of what sort of people should govern schools but alters the proportions, the right combination can be produced by the following formula, taking a governing body of twenty as an example:

Teachers 6
Parents 6
Local Education Authority Representatives 4
Local Community Representatives 4

It will prove a missed opportunity if the pressure that has been mounting during the seventies for parents and teachers to have a greater influence in school government does not lead to their acquiring *effective* power in the eighties. Sadly, the 1980 Education Act does not offer much encouragement, since it provides for only two parents and two teachers on each governing body. What the Act does is make a show of handing over influence without actually doing it.

Such reservations as one has about raising the level of parental and teacher involvement arise from the fear that unrepresentative pressure groups will dominate the situation. Thus teacher power may well mean no more than handing over key decisions to the largest of the teachers' unions in a school. Similarly, parent power may simply mean whoopee for the local branch of the Confederation for the Advancement of State Education. It is perhaps significant that the Advisory Centre for Education – once described by *The Times Educational Supplement* as providing for parents experiencing middle-class anxieties over the education of their children – sees a new role ahead for itself in providing for the parent-governor. Peter Newell, the director, believes that his organization is well placed to offer courses and advice to parents who find themselves governing schools. While schools will stand to benefit from an increase in the part played by parents and teachers in decision making, that will only apply if the new voices which are raised on governing bodies are those of ordinary people whose readiness to listen exceeds their commitment to making sweeping decisions.

The idea of pupils being involved in the work of governing bodies has disturbing implications. The Taylor Report envisages boys and girls of sixteen and upwards being appointed to govern schools; the National Association of Head Teachers, in its response, recommends appointment at eighteen. Both approaches would in effect limit representation to the sixth form, although it would be feasible for some fifth formers – the ones with early birthdays – to be involved under the first scheme.

There are three principal reasons why the notion of pupil-governors deserves to have a large question mark placed beside it.

Firstly, most of those boys and girls whose school days are almost behind them wish to concentrate their attention on passing their examinations and would be wise to do so. In my experience, those most anxious to get into the school government scene are the least typical sixth-formers. They are often distinguishable from the rest by their lack of enthusiasm for the rigours of academic study. The sixties and seventies saw the birth of a new kind of university student – one whose perpetual involvement in the politics of confrontation left him no time to study anything. Perhaps in the eighties we are destined to see the rise of his sixth-form counterpart – the pupil-governor of nineteen or twenty whose destiny it is to be a perpetual A level candidate.

Such a vision is not as unrealistic as it sounds. One may be sure that, should pupil-governors become a reality, there will be those who will remain at school not to learn but to govern. Is it too wild to imagine a few being sponsored and briefed by the National Union of School Students? Those with strong views and deep convictions are inclined to take such opportunities as are available to them. I recollect many years ago asking a young giant at Latymer Upper School why he was staying on. I had expected some answer about subjects to be studied or a university place to be secured, but my assumptions were false. 'Well Sir,' said he of the open countenance and frank blue gaze, 'I'm really only here for the rowing.' By the mid-eighties one might well be hearing something like, 'I'm really only here to help govern the place.'

The second reason for opposition to the pupil-governor concept has to do with the nature and extent of governors' powers. In my view it is unthinkable that one pupil should be in a position to pass judgement on whether or not another should or should not be suspended or expelled; on what other pupils should or should not study and how it should be done; on which members of staff should be promoted and matters of that kind. I have the gravest reservations about an eighteen-year-old being party to any of that, despite the encouragement offered by the largest of the head teachers' professional organizations. With regard to the Taylor proposal that sixteen-year-olds should pass judgement in such matters, it is quite astonishing in its implications. If youngsters of sixteen are thought ready to exercise the powers that the Taylor Report proposes school governors should possess, what possible reason is there for not allowing them to vote in parliamentary elections? Indeed, logic points precisely in the direction of their enfranchisement. If children should have a say in how their schools are run, how much more should they have the right to some part in choosing the government that decides what sort of education system should exist. Yet one suspects there would be some reluctance on the part of the politicians who wish to see Taylor implemented to take the next step and invite children to exercise power at the ballot box.

The third reason for my opposition to pupil involvement in school government is that, contrary to the belief of some of its advocates, it is not the way to teach children about their political responsibilities. In that respect, it is totally misleading, for it makes a promise that it cannot keep. The most that the Taylor proposals offer in terms of genuine political activity in any one school is the chance for a few sixth-formers to attend half a dozen governors' meetings. Significantly, they will almost certainly be about to leave the institution they are governing by the time they have enough experience to make use of their situation. They will certainly not have to live for long with the consequences of those decisions to which they are party. It would be hard to think of anything more unreal and less likely to educate young people in their political responsibilities.

A few years ago there was a question in an Oxford entrance paper that asked, 'Is it possible to imagine a world in which two plus two is not equal to four?' An answer came immediately to my mind: 'Yes, the world of my fourth-year bottom maths set.' The trouble with taking maths with a bottom set is that you have to keep on teaching them the same things. Even if, with much care and no little pain, one communicates some simple rule, half the class will have lost its grip on it again by the next lesson. As a result, there is a temptation to prepare less carefully;

to take the business of teaching less seriously; to deny one's professional responsibility. An identical situation exists in political education. The education system has avoided it because of the fear that it cannot be done successfully. Some schools have abandoned religious education for the same reason, notwithstanding the legal requirement that it should be provided.

Perhaps political education should be required by law. It would certainly make a power of difference to the political behaviour and attitudes of the adult population if there were a better understanding of the way the system operates; of what is possible and what is not; of what the ordinary citizen can do to combat social and economic problems and what he might reasonably expect parliament to do for him. 'What', asked another question in that same Oxford entrance paper, 'do elections in Britain decide?' Some sixth-formers with whom I discussed that showed such a contempt for politicians as made me fear for the future of our democracy. Their dismissal of political people was paradoxically associated with a conviction that only they could do anything about the country's problems. They misunderstood both their own position and that of those they criticized. It is time we grasped the nettle of political education and sorted out the thinking of the next generation of voters. I am not talking about getting the syllabus right for O level British Constitution or A level Government and Politics. If the cause of parliamentary democracy is to be properly understood by young people, it is no good concentrating on those who choose to specialize in the study of it. Indeed, the opposite is the case. We must do something about the vast chasm of ignorance that opens before the feet of nine-tenths of those who leave school at sixteen and march out into a world where power politics hold sway.

Josie was about to leave and would in a couple of years have the vote. I asked the class what a dictator was. Josie did not put her hand up. If she knew something, it had to be announced at once. She knew what a dictator was. 'It's when you write letters with one of them machines.' So much for Eltham Green's brand of political education. But we do try. Everyone in the fourth and fifth follows a programme in human relations which includes politics. Some of the governors were suspicious when we introduced it, and there has been a good deal of trouble about some parts of it. In 1979, the chairman of the Labour Party demanded that we desist from teaching the children about NATO. But there has been no opposition to our political curriculum from parents. What is more important, the boys and girls are very enthusiastic about it. They will certainly learn more from it than from the sort of involvement in school government offered by the Taylor recommendations.

It has been suggested in some quarters that the majority of the proposals contained in the Taylor Report are unlikely to come to pass now that a new Education Act has established the position regarding school government for the forseeable future. Taylor, it is argued, is destined to gather dust on the shelves of the Department of Education and Science, like so many reports on education which have preceded it. That is a mistaken view for two reasons. Firstly, the 1980 Education Act in no way alters the situation whereby the functions to be exercised by the separate elements of school government – local education authority, governors and head teacher – are determined by articles of government drawn up by the first named. Secondly, while the Act falls a long way short of the Taylor recommendations regarding membership of governing bodies, the tenth of twelve clauses in the section dealing with this subject states: 'Nothing in this section shall be construed as preventing the inclusion in the governing body of any school of governors additional to those required by this section.' The way is clear for any local education authority to go all the way down the road laid by those who made up the Taylor Committee.

If even half the changes that are afoot regarding the powers of the head teacher and the composition and function of school governing bodies come to fruition in the eighties, the decade will call for a new kind of head markedly different from any known in the past. Those who have in the seventies been concerned to make proposals about this or that change of structure, have declined to state in specific terms what shall in consequence be the precise role of the head. It seems his constitutional position is to be left ill-defined. He will no longer be a man whose special role in the day-to-day running of things distinguishes him from his governors, who have general oversight. Under the 1980 Education Act, he becomes *ex-officio* a governor of his school unless he positively elects otherwise. Behind this lies the assumption, derived from the Taylor Report, that he should have one vote worth no more than anyone else's and that his position should cease to be regarded as an especially authoritative one.

It will be interesting to see what sort of people emerge to fill this new role. Equally interesting will be the way in which the established guard adapt to new conditions. One suspects that it will not take less than a decade for the new kind of head to be clearly distinguishable. Those who hold what is in effect the most powerful position in the education system will not surrender their ground readily.

Nine

Measuring Success

It was once said of General Douglas Macarthur that he never consulted anyone before telling God what to do. In this, it was claimed, he was unlike the Cabots and the Lodges, who discussed things among themselves before issuing instructions to the Almighty.

It is a common weakness of schools in general and of head teachers in particular that they do not take too readily to the idea that their judgement is less than omnipotent. Seeing the reaction of many teachers to criticism, one would never think they spent their days encouraging people to think for themselves. It is no wonder that pressure has been mounting throughout the seventies for some form of assessment and accountability to be applied to the performance of schools.

In July 1978, ninety-four head teachers and thirty-six inspectors gathered at Avery Hill College for the annual conference of Inner London comprehensive heads who were to spend three days examining the role of the head teacher in the eighties. There was no doubt which session was anticipated with the greatest interest. The final speaker was to be Professor Michael Rutter who, it was assumed, would give a preview of his research findings into the actual effects of secondary schools upon the children attending them. It was with a keen sense of anticipation that the conference delegates heard him announce that he had discovered what made a good secondary school. Everyone waited with enthusiasm to hear the characteristics of his or her own establishment described. Only the most paranoic felt threatened. The successful secondary school, the speaker explained, was one with a tight structure, firm discipline, streaming and setting, school uniform, and a commitment to similar traditional approaches. He developed this theme further. A successful secondary school was one with a flexible structure, no great emphasis on discipline, mixed ability teaching, no school uniform, and a progressive approach to educational issues. Could one have it both ways? Indeed, one could. The truth which the Rutter Report put forward on its publication a year after the conference was blindingly obvious when one thought about it. What makes a school successful is not its organization but its ethos. It is not what you do, but the way that you do it that matters most. Style and atmosphere are more important than particular methods.

Research had revealed that the same actions by teachers led to quite different results in different schools. 'For example, if children were left alone in lessons to get on with their work, in some schools they did just that. In others, any relaxation of direct control led to an increase in disruptive behaviour. It appeared there was something about the way children were dealt with in general which influenced their behaviour even when there was no direct supervision of staff.'

Teachers all have their own opinions about how to influence the way children behave when they are out of sight. Some say it is done by the strict enforcement of high standards when they are present so that children become conditioned to behaving themselves. Others say it is done by allowing a good deal of freedom so that children discover the advantages of self-discipline. One thing is clear: there are first-class teachers and third-raters in both groups. What makes the difference is the relationship between teacher and taught, which may have little or nothing to do with the method employed. The best teachers move from one method to another between different classes and age groups. Some pupils develop best under firm handling; others need to stretch their wings quite early on.

The American political writer Theodore White tells how ambitious politicians used to watch John F. Kennedy when he was addressing a meeting in the hope of spotting his secret. They would lick their lips anxiously and lean forward in their seats, attempting to discern the special trick the great man was playing which they had somehow failed to acquire. There are some miserably unsuccessful teachers – and few miseries are greater than the life of a bad teacher – who believe there is some special trick which is the key to classroom achievement.

A man who had spent nearly ten desperate years in the classroom sat in my study one day, his head in his hands. 'Just tell me,' he said, 'what I'm doing wrong.' It would have been easy to say that he should stop shouting at the class, but he had tried the quiet approach with no success. I might have told him to talk less himself and ask more questions, but my colleagues and I had witnessed the chaos that reigned if he tried to have a discussion. More careful use of the blackboard? His blackboard work was far better than mine. More careful marking of written exercises? He spent more time marking than most teachers I have known. More careful attention to punctuality, so that he arrived first at his classroom and was in control from the start? He was always so terrified of getting there to find anarchy already established that he literally ran from the staffroom at lesson change.

The man concerned had tried every teaching method ever thought of, and a few the educational researchers have not yet arrived at, like actually kneeling down in front of a class and begging them to shut up. None was of any avail, because he had one fundamental and insuperable weakness: the inability to make relationships with young people. For lack of that, many a good man has bitten the classroom dust. No amount of attention to *method* will solve that basic inadequacy of *style*. That is not to say there are not techniques to be learned and methods to be mastered if one is to become an effective educator. But, in the end, the medium is the message.

There is a Zulu proverb that says, 'I cannot hear the words you are saying because what you *are* shouts so loudly in my ears.' That applies both to the individual teacher and to the school as a social institution. As the Rutter findings have shown, it is the social climate in a school that determines the effectiveness of what goes on inside the walls, not the organizational details. It is the quality of life that shouts in our ears.

So what are the ingredients of success? What common characteristics are to be found in effective schools of different styles? Michael Rutter and his colleagues have nothing new to tell us, but they remind us of some important old truths which have become somewhat neglected. Three of them seem to me especially significant. Firstly, effective education will take place where lessons require children to work hard and where the individual teacher is both strongly supported and closely supervised by senior staff. Secondly, the teacher who provides a good model of behaviour will generate high standards of conduct among those he teaches. Thirdly, a school with firm leadership at all levels of decision-making will be more successful than one in which policies are hard to discern and lacking in vigorous application. Hearing the news that President Calvin Coolidge had died, one journalist asked, 'How could they tell?' It is a question that might be asked about the leadership of some schools.

There are two important things to be observed about the three features mentioned. Firstly, they may be applied equally to schools that are organized in vastly different ways. Commitment to this or that way of teaching or to this or that range of rewards and punishments is neither here nor there. Secondly, the key to success lies in the quality and suitability of people in the teaching profession. 'One of the common responses of practitioners to any piece of research,' writes Michael Rutter, 'is that it seems to be a tremendous amount of hard work just to demonstrate what we knew already on the basis of experience or common sense.' One is reminded of Winston Churchill's statement about his war speeches. He was, he said, merely giving utterance to what everyone knew and felt. His role was simply to supply the British lion with a roar.

Of all the roaring truths contained in the Rutter Report of 1979, none brings more comfort to good teachers than the conclusion that schools can and do make a difference to the way children develop. 'The family', said Michael Rutter at that Avery Hill conference, 'is the most important influence in children's development.' No one will argue with that. But the effect of schooling is both extensive and profound, and that is now part of the accepted body of educational knowledge for the eighties thanks to his report, *Fifteen Thousand Hours*.

The definition of success used in the book is a relatively narrow one, concentrating on four things: pupils' attendance, their behaviour in school, their results in public examinations, and their delinquency out of school. The influence of school on the first three was found to be considerable. One thereby arrives at the following definition of a good school: it is one where most pupils attend regularly, behave themselves and pass their examinations. Most people would probably settle for that.

On 23 March 1978, London Weekend Television devoted *The London Programme* to the Rutter Report, comparing the liberal style of Islington Green School under Margaret Maden with the rather more teutonic approach used at Eltham Green. A subsequent local newspaper report read as follows:

At Eltham Green there is streaming (separation of pupils of different ability levels), some corporal punishment for boys, and no pupil participation in the running of the school. At Islington Green, there is mixed-ability teaching, no corporal punishment, and the pupils participate in the running of the school. Professor Rutter's view was that none of these points were decisive. What the schools had in common was a well worked out and unified approach to education, consistency in discipline, punctuality by the teachers and a caring attitude to children.

In advance of the event, there were those who were worried about allowing television cameras into the school, but Gavin Weightman and his team from LWT caused no problems and presented a genuine, accurate and balanced picture of life at Eltham Green. In my experience, the media will only report you wrongly if you allow it to happen that way. It is a theme that needs developing, for schools have miles to go before they can sleep easy on this question. The issue is a critical one, since a school's success is to some extent both measured and determined by what the papers say.

There was a time long ago when a head teacher could ignore the media. The headmaster of the ancient grammar school in which my teaching career began considered it below his dignity to respond to press inquiries. Getting into the newspapers was a fate worse than death, except once a year at prizegiving. It was no business of newspaper people to be poking around in the world of education.

But the days when one could get away with a policy of disdainful silence are over and gone. If the head will not speak to reporters, they will be at the gate chatting up pupils to get a story from them. What is more, the pupils will be prepared to talk. Any questioning of their right to be photographed and to declare their position on routine subjects like homosexuality among teachers, pregnancy rates in the sixth form, or last week's knife fight behind the gym will bring immediate protests from (a) parents, (b) half the school governors and (c) the local branch of the National Council for Civil Liberties. It is no good asking what Arnold of Rugby would make of it all. He is dead and gone, like the notion that what happened in the playground yesterday is not a matter of legitimate interest to people outside the school.

It will do the education system no harm for people to hear more of the real problems schools have to face these days. The defensiveness of head teachers serves no good purpose. If we all admitted that (a) schools have become violent places and (b) head teachers have no adequate means of dealing with the teenage hooligan, we might get something done about the rising tide of corridor crime. When I was first appointed a headmaster, an inspector advised me to respond to the press as I would to a driver whose car I might have bumped into. 'Never admit anything,' was his counsel. It is the worst possible approach, being guaranteed to generate suspicion and mistrust.

Newspapers, radio and television are among the most powerful agencies for passing on accurate information about the education system in a way that catches public attention. It was the media that translated the great education debate of the late seventies into issues that ordinary people could understand. In my opinion, Sue MacGregor has done more through her *Woman's Hour* discussions on educational topics to inform average parents about the real substance of issues than most teachers would ever be able to do. And don't tell me the programme only gets through to the female half of the population. Whenever I have taken part, fathers of Eltham Green pupils have told me how they just happened to hear me although it was to be understood they didn't normally listen to broadcasts for women. By chance, the car radio happened to be on, or the wife had the kitchen radio turned up rather loudly. I wonder if Miss MacGregor knows she has half the male population at her feet.

In one of the 1965 Guildhall Lectures, jointly sponsored by Granada Television and the British Association, Alistair Cooke talked about the impact of the media upon modern society. He began by describing an incident when he stood on the edge of the Sahara Desert and watched a camel driver riding towards him from the far distance. As the man came closer, Alistair Cooke noticed that he was in a half-bent position with something held to his ear. It was a transistor radio. From it there echoed across the sands of Africa the voice of Frank Sinatra asking the world a question: 'All of me, why not take all of me?' With consummate skill, Cooke went on to illustrate the impact of radio and television on the way the developing countries of the East see the prosperous ones of the West; and on the way in which the have-nots of the Western world see themselves in relation to the signs of wealth that are all around them:

> Remote peoples who once knew nothing beyond the horizon are now getting the beginnings of a universal education . . . They hear that what is wrong with their eyes is tachoma and what is wrong with their baby is beri-beri or yaws. They have long known they were sick, but they now know that they are poor and that it is not written in the stars that they and their generations must be so . . .

I suppose that if you sit in a mean room most of the day with a litter of listless children and a worn-down mother, and you keep seeing the svelte girls in the automobile ads and the young white Apollos, and the chatty glowing families, and the house in the pines secured by a mortgage from the silvery-haired saint in the friendly bank – I suppose you come to believe that this is the way the whites live. They have everything, not only the vote and the clean jobs, and the mathematics, if you're interested – but all the goodies and the money and the golden girls. It must get to be unbearable . . .

Whether the ultimate influence of the mass media is for good or ill, they have had and are having the profoundest political effects around the world . . . they have disclosed the rich world to the poor world, acquainted the poor with their own poverty and both by accident and design, but surely by endless dinning repetition, massaged the discontent and revolutionary instincts of the dispossessed. Ladies and gentlemen, you have been warned.

The education system should heed the warning. Local education authorities and schools must accept that during the seventies the media have acquired an interest in reporting educational matters well beyond anything that was general in earlier decades. There is a sense in which the press, television and radio are doing for education what Alistair Cooke talked about – informing those who are exploited and manipulated that it is not written in the stars that it must be so. One illustration will serve to make the point.

In 1978, Eltham Green's oversubscription reached fairly dramatic proportions with 429 applicants for 330 places. In fact, there had been even more applicants the year before, but I had agreed to an ILEA request to take an extra form and that had more or less solved the problem. Most parents had been prepared to accept a second choice of school, while those who most wanted Eltham Green had got it. It had seemed a sensible accommodation and, anticipating a repetition in 1978, I had very early on offered to repeat the exercise. However, while it was one thing for us to take extra pupils when it was part of the administrators' intended scheme of things, it was quite another matter when they had something else in mind. My offer was not accepted and trouble loomed.

'Storm over Schools Allocation' shouted one local newspaper headline above an account of a meeting between the education officer and disgruntled parents. 'Outsiders get Places at Top School' said another – a reference to the fact that children from a neighbouring division had been given places that Eltham parents thought should have gone to their children. When the new school year opened in the autumn, fifteen parents kept their youngsters out of school. I repeated my offer to the ILEA to provide extra places. Under the headline 'Head Battles for Lost Children of Rebel Parents', my view of the situation was quoted: 'It is my professional opinion that a child's success depends upon his enthusiasm for his school and his parents' support for it. That being so, every effort should be made to meet the wishes of parents.' But the Inner London Education Authority was, like the parents, digging in, and the same report carried the official response: 'We do not propose to overcrowd one school when there are places available at other schools.' It was not, of course, the way the administrators had seen things twelve months earlier.

The growing anxiety of the local education authority over the effect of our situation on others was understandable. The success of one school in the matter of recruitment will often spell trouble for another: a point already made in chapter six. This was precisely the position with regard to the relationship between Eltham Green and a neighbouring comprehensive which had established and maintained a reputation second to none in the sixties. As the tide of popularity turned in the seventies, problems were inevitable. It had always been assumed that the balance of influence between the two schools would never change. The fact that it had happened was greeted with astonishment, jubilation and remorse in different quarters and in about equal proportions. The 1978 storm brought the rumblings of almost a decade to a climax.

As the noise of conflict raged throughout the autumn,

newspaper headlines describing Eltham Green's situation followed the drama with no lack of enthusiasm. 'Girl Battles for School Place' was the mid-October message. Fortuitously, someone left the school and one little girl was admitted after having missed the first half of the autumn term. This made other parents even more determined, and two boys were brought to the school in full Eltham Green uniform. Despite my protests, I was instructed by the divisional officer to send them away, an event that earned the headline 'Outcasts' from Tony Doran in the *Evening News*. Under a picture of two sad little boys outside our school gate appeared a statement by a spokesman for the local education authority which splendidly summed up the attitude of the bureaucracy. London schools, it was unequivocally asserted, 'are managed by the education officer and not by the head and governors. It is up to us to decide whether a school is full or not and who should go there.' That brief but devastating revelation of official thinking about where the power should lie in the education system put teachers, parents and school governors firmly in their place. By November there was a front-page headline in the *Eltham Times* which said 'Rebel Parent ready to go to Prison', followed by another a few weeks later declaring 'MP wants Probe on ILEA Action'. At the end of the month an editorial entitled 'How Much Choice?' put its finger on the question that lay at the heart of the matter.

The story did not end until the following spring, when I was finally given permission to take in the children whose parents had waited nine months for places. There were not vacancies for them all, but officialdom suddenly decided to give way. There was an important tactical reason why they had waited so long. Between February and April 1979, parents of local primary school children were choosing secondary schools for their youngsters. The unwisdom of choosing Eltham Green had to be demonstrated quite clearly. By continuing to make an example of the previous year's parents who had refused to do as they were told, the administrators hoped to avoid a repetition of events. By the time May came, the danger of that was past, and officials felt free to change their position in order to avoid the unpleasant press publicity which would follow legal action against the recalcitrant group for not sending their children to school. By now, some of the parents were demanding to know why they had not been prosecuted. It was a good question, since everyone knew that the Inner London Education Authority's case had little chance of succeeding in a court of law. It was a near certainty that the judiciary would award the parents places for their children at Eltham Green, especially as the head of the school had declared his readiness to have them. A defeat in the courts would mean that people like head teachers and parents could indeed have some influence on school placements.

Bernard Levin has said of the opera *Pelléas et Mélisande* that it has a built-in happy ending for him, the mere fact that the thing has ended being quite sufficient to make him happy. There was a good deal had been achieved. That was almost entirely attributable to two related factors: the determination of parents, and the attention given to their situation by the media. In the year reached. However, seen in the context of subsequent events, a good deal had been achieved. It was almost entirely attributable to two related factors: the determination of parents, and the attention given to their situation by the media. In the year immediately following the events described, the reservation of places at Eltham Green School for children in the neighbouring division was removed. All 1979 applications from the area of Eltham from which the main body of insistent parents came in 1978 were successful. Anyone who makes a coincidence of that does not know how fearful local education authorities are of media criticism. But the implications of the media coverage were not merely local. Without doubt these events – together with others like them elsewhere in the country – had an influence on the contents of the 1980 Education Act which says:

> Every local education authority shall make arrangements for enabling the parents of a child to appeal against any decision made by or on behalf of the authority as to the school at which education is to be provided for the child in the exercise of the authority's functions . . . The decision of an appeal committee

on any such appeal shall be binding on the local education
authority . . .

Measuring a school's success in terms of sympathetic media
treatment is not an idea that appeals to some professional
educators, but it is part of modern reality. If a head teacher
cannot explain what he is doing in a way that can be reported in
a supportive and understanding way, he is either a bad
communicator or he is running his school badly. When I took a
few thrashings from the newspapers as a young headmaster, it
was because I had not worked out clearly in my own mind what
I was about. In my very first newspaper interview after
appointment, I made a thorough mess of things. I had just come
down from a Liverpool comprehensive at which mixed ability
teaching was used through the school. Foolishly, I mentioned
this early on and allowed the reporter to concentrate almost the
entire interview on the subject. I emerged on the front page of
the local paper the next week as a progressive messiah who had
come to build an unstreamed kingdom at Eltham Green.
Nothing could have been further from the truth, but the fault
was mine.

After a time, I learned the secret of good newspaper, television
and radio coverage. The important thing is not to be tied to the
questions one is asked, since those doing the asking rarely
understand the issues. One must reach beyond the questioner to
those who will be listening or watching or reading one's words.
After a Thames Television discussion about public examinations,
one of the other participants said to me, with great irritation,
'We didn't talk about the real issues.' There was only one reply:
'Then why on earth didn't you raise them?'

Of course, sometimes one has to face the unexpected. I was
asked early in 1979 by the BBC if I would take part in a
programme for the International Year of the Child to do with
children's rights in school. There would be a studio discussion
involving myself, a couple of other adults, and one or two young
schoolchildren. It sounded reasonable, so I agreed. Subsequently,
I was informed that there would not be any children after all.

Later still, I learned that the two adults would in fact be John Munford from the National Union of School Students, plus someone else from the same organization. By now it was clear that things were not as they had at first appeared. It was an opinion confirmed when the pre-recorded opening sequence of the programme was run as a preamble to our discussion: there was John Munford proclaiming the policies of the NUSS for all the world like a party political broadcaster.

Every newspaper I saw that reviewed the programme – from the *Daily Telegraph* to the *Kentish Independent* – highlighted one particular sentence which I had used in addressing the sixteen-year-old *éminence grise* of the NUSS: 'You are a most presumptuous young man.' So thoroughly did the proceedings succeed in polarizing opinions that it has been shown several times.

In February 1980, a television programme in the *Open Door* series entitled *Carry on Comprehensives* drew its own picture of the successful comprehensive school. It was characterized by, among other things, a disposition towards mixed ability teaching, a high level of staff consultation, and a willingness on the part of staff to be on first-name terms with senior pupils. In short, the successful school was one in which egalitarianism was the basis of the structure and organization. The case was impressively presented by Dame Margaret Miles on behalf of the Campaign for Comprehensive Education. Without doubt, many enthusiasts would embrace its assumptions. They would argue that, if the comprehensive fails to alter the social structure and to make for a higher level of integration between children of different abilities and backgrounds, it has failed in its prime purpose. But there is growing evidence that pupils tend to remain with those of their own social group when left free to do so, whatever organizational structure one builds. Juliette Ford's research gave rise to early suspicions about this, and others have since confirmed her findings. The most strikingly obvious example of children's disinclination to be integrated is presented by the behaviour of ethnic and racial groups. Looking out of the window into the playground at break or in the lunch hour, one sees the West Indian boys playing together and the West Indian girls talking together. In lessons — whether they be streamed, setted or mixed — ethnic pairing as often as not underlies who sits with whom. Similarly, the bright children of educated parents are inclined to associate with one another, as are the boys and girls who have learning problems. Of course, all of this merely reflects the society in which schools operate and serves to illustrate what a massive task faces anyone who sets out to change the existing pattern of relationships in any community. The issue becomes a contentious one when it appears that the drive towards social change impedes academic performance. While mixed ability teaching may promote social justice, is it able at the same time to maintain educational standards?

While extensive and intensive staff consultation makes for democracy, what is the outcome in terms of the classroom situation? The programme *Carry on Comprehensives* emphasized how the good comprehensive would not dream of trying to get by with one staff meeting a term, which was the way of doing things in the old selectives. Some would say we have gone too far in the other direction. After several lengthy meetings about the lower school curriculum at one school, a head of department indicated at the start of yet another coming together on the same subject that he had a motion to offer. 'I propose,' he said, 'that today we *decide* something.' It is a characteristic of schools that rapid decisions are frequently called for in the running of them. Conversely, it is a characteristic of teachers that, where two or three are gathered together, they will each find a different point of view to expound, as often as not at great length. Reaching decisions by the consensus approach is only possible in two ways: by having staff spend long hours in meetings after school, or by reducing teaching programmes so that discussions may take place while the school is in session. Whether the massive amount of time given to the consultative process in some large comprehensives invariably has a positive outcome is highly questionable. But some would say that is not the point: the very existence of a democratic structure is self-justifying. It is a view that follows logically from the ideas expounded in *Half Way*

There, the prospectus of the comprehensive school movement drawn up by Mrs Caroline Wedgwood Benn and Professor Brian Simon. Of the thirty-one conditions prescribed for the creating of a successful comprehensive school, the great majority have to do one way or another with the promotion of equality and democracy. While some have a direct relationship to the classroom situation, others have nothing to do with it. For example, not only must all forms of setting and streaming be abolished, but there must be an elected student council.

Not all those who have chosen to teach in comprehensive schools see their main purpose as social engineering. It follows that different professionals – not to mention those outside the actual school situation – will look for different things in attempting to measure success. Indeed, the picture becomes immensely confused when one realizes that what one teacher would regard as a sign of success another would mark down as a sign of failure. For example, some regard sixth-form conformity as a welcome sign of a return to high standards, while others condemn it as a mark of arrested development.

'A faith,' wrote Arthur Koestler in his contribution to the book *The God that Failed*, 'is not acquired by reason. One does not fall in love with a woman, or enter the womb of a church, as a result of logical persuasion. Reason may defend an act of faith – but only after the act has been committed, and the man committed to the act.' The same applies to any person's assessment of what makes a school successful. Those parents who tell me what a good school Eltham Green is – and those who say the opposite – do not really understand the finer points of subject setting or the relative merits and demerits of our present horizontal pastoral system as against the vertical one which was once used. The first group might say, if questioned, that they prefer setting to mixed ability teaching and are attracted to a year system rather than a house system – but the reasons they would give would almost certainly be ones offered to them by senior staff at an earlier stage. Frequently, parents will rationalize their approval or disapproval of a school by seizing upon some organizational feature, or something that appears easy to measure, like examination statistics or how well or badly the children behave in the street. But how people feel about a school does not really depend upon such things. When Kingsdale School at Dulwich got into the news as a result of a bus inspector being hit in the eye with a brick, the resultant publicity merely served to confirm existing opinions, namely, that the school was a centre of disorder and violence or, if you were one of its sympathizers, that a good school was being misrepresented for the umpteenth time (the assailant turned out not to be a Kingsdale boy). People make up their minds, then look for the evidence to confirm their feelings.

So, what does give people the feelings they have about a particular institution? We return to more or less where this chapter began, to Professor Michael Rutter's identification of ethos as the key factor in marking out successful schools. Different people look for very different things in any educational institution, but those which recruit successfully and are held in high regard have one thing in common: an identifiable way of going about things which is plain to see and which has the consent and support of the great majority of those associated with them.

Professor Rutter saw firm leadership as one of the chief characteristics subserving the notion of ethos. The unoriginality of such a proposition does nothing to reduce its significance. Its implications grow in importance when one considers the new style of school government likely to emerge in the eighties. One of the great traditions of the English education system has been the distinctive role of the head teacher in establishing the success of a school. By the end of the eighties, that way of doing things may well have disappeared from the state sector.

Ten

Conclusion

The eighties will be a period of contraction for the education service. There will be fewer children, fewer teachers, and fewer schools than in the seventies. Those institutions which are least successful are more at risk than at any time since the passing of the 1944 Education Act.

But that is not to say that risk has not been the companion of schools for a long time. As the problems of a new decade loom ahead, one may be inclined to forget the threatening conditions which were present ten years ago in the spring of 1970, when I assumed the headship of Eltham Green School. Risinghill had died only five years earlier, and the debate about that particular act of execution still raged. It was fuelled by a book that did not appear until 1968, three years after the event, but which produced one of the most intense educational debates of the century and one that stirred emotions more deeply than the great debate of the late seventies. Leila Berg's *Risinghill: Death of a Comprehensive School* earned an accolade from Robin Pedley, at that time Professor of Education at Exeter, which no professional educator could ignore:

> Perhaps once in a generation a book appears whose power and passion, clarity and courage, match the great social issue with which it deals. Dickens achieved such a masterpiece in *Nicholas Nickleby*, but professional educationalists have been less successful. It has been left to Leila Berg . . . to turn a brilliant searchlight on one of the saddest and most sickening episodes in the history of English education. The book is a powerful and passionate indictment of prejudice, bureaucracy and conservatism

in high places . . . it puts the most powerful local education authority in the country in the dock. The great reputation of the publishers is behind this courageous decision, ensuring that Risinghill must become a *cause célèbre*. As a result, we may yet atone in some measure to the betrayed children who cried in the lavatories on the day that Risinghill was closed.

The opposing view to this *Sunday Times* review of 28 April 1968 appeared just a few days later in the *Times Educational Supplement* in the form of its 3 May editorial. 'A great deal of nonsense has been written about Risinghill School,' said the opening sentence. Leila Berg's book was 'biased, inaccurate and unfair'. One of the principal reasons for closure was unarguable and made the action thoroughly justified: the school was 'clearly unpopular with parents as compared with other schools in the neighbourhood'. There were not enough parents 'prepared to support Mr Duane's type of education'. John Brown, who had conducted a distinguished and successful headship at Sedgehill School for nearly twelve years, wrote to the *Sunday Times* in the same vein, pointing out that Risinghill's failure to recruit pupils demanded that some action be taken.

None can pretend that these issues are over and done with. Given the competitive conditions that will apply between one school and another in the eighties, who will prophecy that recruitment will not once again become the key to survival? Since it was one of Eltham Green's principal problems in 1970, it was perhaps not surprising that the Risinghill debate – which was still continuing at that time – seemed to have a certain relevance to my own particular situation and prospects. There is a very obvious sense in which this book is a natural successor to *Risinghill: Death of a Comprehensive School*, in that it tells the other side of the story. Had Eltham Green failed to solve its massive recruitment problems in the early seventies, its future would without doubt have come in for very close scrutiny.

The destiny of the most famous comprehensive of them all, Kidbrooke, provides an object lesson. By the second half of the seventies, the school was having immense difficulty in attracting the three hundred and ninety girls a year who were supposed to make up its annual intake. In consequence, its designated recruitment was reduced by stages to three hundred; but in 1978 there were only one hundred and fifty-six applicants at first-choice stage for the places available. With the effect of the reduced birthrate of the late sixties arriving to exacerbate the school's recruitment problems, some dramatic action was called for. When news of what was to happen in 1980 first leaked out, it was greeted with disbelief. The idea that what had once been Dame Mary Green's distinctive and distinguished comprehensive academy for girls might become a mixed school had never occurred to some people – least of all to many of the parents who had sent their daughters there. By all accounts, some stormy meetings ensued. Making the school mixed was, however, the obvious solution, since it opened up a whole new field of recruitment.

It is interesting to reflect on what would have been the fate of Eltham Green if its situation in 1970, which was not very different from that of Kidbrooke eight years later, had not changed beyond recognition during the early and middle years of that decade. But the battle for survival is not yet won. Indeed, no school can be sure of its future in the years ahead. Eltham Green's success is now beginning to rebound upon it as local education authority administrators put pressure on primary school head teachers not to allow parents to choose the school for their children.

The instructions offered in 1980 were fairly specific. Primary heads were asked to take note of the 'constraints that are encountered with regards to placements at Eltham Green' while bearing in mind with respect to the neighbouring comprehensive mentioned on page 175 that 'it would be prudent for parents living in the vicinity . . . to consider this school very carefully as a first preference.' A nod is as good as a wink, and those receiving it acted accordingly. In the first week of parental interviews at primary schools, I was rung up by an agitated mother who said, 'I told my daughter's head teacher I wanted Eltham Green and he said no, no, no. I wasn't allowed to choose your school and, if I did, he would write on the form that he had told me I mustn't.' She had a question that provided a devastating comment on the claims of the ILEA to allow parents freedom of choice: 'Will I get into trouble if I say it's to be Eltham Green?'

As well as pressure by the bureaucracy on those who guide the choices parents make, the media coverage which inspired some parents to insist on having a genuine choice during our triumphal march through the late seventies has had the effect of discouraging those of less determined intent. Paradoxically, as falling rolls in the eighties create a situation in which parents ought to be more able than before to have what they want, the likelihood is that things will work in the opposite direction. Because of pressure from teachers' professional associations to reduce the size and/or alter the organization of schools rather than close some of them, it will not be possible for local education authorities to allow consumers to dictate the situation. There has recently appeared on the Inner London scene a new educational phenomenon in the form of the federal school. Under the headmastership of Michael Marland, North Westminster School combines three existing schools, all of which have shrunk to a fraction of their former size. The advantages of federation have been spelled out by the pioneer head:

> This is the first school in London to be organized on these particular lines: a linked school with three sites. It will retain small local schools, near to home for the younger children, and combine them with a more adult community for the older pupils in a separate building. It can provide us with the best of both worlds – large-scale facilities but small-scale communities. Each unit will be a community in itself, while the whole school will span the area in which the children live and promote links with the community.

One wonders what on earth all the fuss used to be over the split-site comprehensive. Finding a way to justify on educational grounds what is politically convenient and economically necessary offers no little relief to a local education authority which – like all the others in the kingdom – has some hard decisions to make about which schools should survive.

It was suggested in the opening pages of this book that what was about to be written was neither history nor educational philosophy but simply an account of a school's pilgrimage to survival. It is a journey that many schools will take in the new conditions of the eighties, although perhaps for different reasons and along a different route from the one followed by Eltham Green in the last ten years.

In the 1968 edition of the Eltham Green School magazine, fourth-former Christine French had a poem no less riveting than Leila Berg's publication of the same year:

> If I were the sun
> And I saw the things which people had done
> I would eclipse myself
> For ever.

The poem was reproduced the following year by three members of staff in an English textbook they devised entitled *Conflict*. It was a word that aptly summarized the condition of the school on my arrival not long afterwards. Perhaps Christine's poem had been a comment on what she saw around her in classroom and playground, as well as on the condition of the world at large.

It was my resolve in 1970 to get to the bottom of some of Eltham Green's problems or to leave within a year. Often, during those first terrifying twelve months, I observed to the senior master, 'I do not think it can be done.' It was perhaps a measure of how far we came in ten years that, on the third day of the spring term in January 1980, his successor inadvertently reprimanded the school plumber for not wearing school uniform and did not get a back-answer.

The Viking god Woden, after whom we name the middle day of the week, was alleged to be very good at answering men's problems. But his wisdom in human affairs was not secured without a struggle, since truth was stored in the waters of a well guarded by a demon. The story made Wednesday an altogether appropriate day for my appointment to the headship of Eltham Green. It was on that day of the week – in November 1969 – that the post was offered and, with some elation, accepted. On all such occasions, there is a period of euphoria before reality sobers the spirit. The nature of what lay ahead was brought home forcefully by friends in the school's catchment area who stopped me in the street to ask if I had any idea what I was getting into. The Methodist equivalent of a bishop questioned my sanity. A respected professional acquaintance gave the *coup de grâce* to my enthusiasm: 'Eltham Green is hell and it will destroy you.'

But it was not, and it did not. The demon of disorder lurking there was fierce, but could be frightened away. He might at any time return, for he is as immortal as man's inclination to follow the broad road to destruction.

The road from Bomb Alley was a narrow one. Those who read this book will not find much that is original in it. The way to bring order to a school community which has lost its sense of direction and purpose is not hard to discern. It is not knowing what to do but having the determination to do it that presents the problem. That is the truth for what lies ahead as well as what has gone before. The road we travel, if it be the right one, stretches straight and true.